by David Edgar

"I swear by Almighty God

[or do solemnly and truly declare and affirm]

that, on becoming a British citizen, I will be faithful and bear

true allegiance to Her Majesty Queen Elizabeth the Second,

Her Heirs and Successors according to law.

I will give my loyalty to the United Kingdom and respect

its rights and freedoms. I will uphold its democratic values.

I will observe its laws faithfully and fulfill my duties and

obligations as a British citizen."

Testing the Echo was researched and developed through workshops held in 2007. The actors in the workshops were Geraldine Alexander, Teresa Banham, David Beames, Kirsty Bushell, Babou Ceesay, Heather Craney, Ayesha Dharker, Ian Dunn, Matthew Dunster, Farzana Dua Elahe, Joel Fry, Dolya Gavanski, Lloyd Hutchinson, Perveen Hussain, Kika Markham, Lucian Msamati, Chiké Okonkwe, Olivia Poulet, Ian Redford, Sirine Saba, Amit Shah, Christop[...] [...]e grateful to all those who talked to us and for th[...] [...]rick, Abdul-Rehman Malik, Patrick Molloy, Louise [...] [...]nstitute of Race Relations.

Testing the ECHO

Tour 2008

17 – 25 January
Salisbury Playhouse
01722 320333
www.salisburyplayhouse.com

31 January – 2 February
**De Koninklijke Schouwburg
(Royal Theatre of The Hague)**
www.ks.nl

6 – 9 February
Traverse Theatre, Edinburgh
0131 228 1404
www.traverse.co.uk

12 – 16 February
Liverpool Playhouse
0151 709 4776
www.everymanplayhouse.com

19– 23 February
Warwick Arts Centre
024 7652 4524
www.warwickartscentre.co.uk

26 February – 1 March
Guildford's Yvonne Arnaud Theatre
01483 44 00 00
www.yvonne-arnaud.co.uk

11 – 15 March
Library Theatre, Manchester
0161 236 7110
www.librarytheatre.com

18 – 22 March
Oxford Playhouse
01865 305305
www.oxfordplayhouse.com

26 – 29 March
**Theatre Royal,
Bury St Edmunds**
01284 769 505
www.theatreroyal.org

1 April – 3 May
Tricycle Theatre, London
020 7328 1000
www.tricycle.co.uk

7 – 10 May
Birmingham Repertory Theatre
0121 236 4455
www.birmingham-rep.co.uk

Testing the Echo was first performed at
Salisbury Playhouse on 17 January 2008

Chicken Tikka Massala is now a true British national dish, not only because it is the most popular, but because it is a perfect illustration of the way Britain absorbs and adapts external influences. Chicken Tikka is an Indian dish. The Massala sauce was added to satisfy the desire of British people to have their meat served in gravy.

Robin Cook, 19 April 2001

The Company

Emma/Bernie	**Teresa Banham**
Tetyana/Pauline/Halima	**Kirsty Bushell**
Mahmood/Ian/Dragoslav	**Sushil Chudasama**
Muna/Jasminka	**Farzana Dua Elahe**
Aziz/Chong/Toby/Samir	**Ian Dunn**
Martin/Mayor/Ranjit/Derek	**Robert Gwilym**
Jamal/Joshua/Baba	**Syrus Lowe**
Assistant/Chloe/Nasim	**Sirine Saba**

Other parts played by members of the company.

Director	**Matthew Dunster**
Designer	**Paul Wills**
Lighting designer	**Philip Gladwell**
Sound designer	**Ian Dickinson**
Projections designer	**Thomas Gray**
Assistant director	**Naomi Jones**
Casting director	**Louis Hammond**
Dialect coach	**Sally Hague**
Costume supervisor	**Jackie Orton**
Production manager	**Gary Beestone** for Giraffe
Tour production manager	**Gareth Edwards** for Giraffe
Producer	**Rebecca Pilbeam**
Company stage manager	**Xenia Lewis**
Deputy stage manager	**Danni Bastian**
Assistant stage manager	**Maggie Bradley**
Wardrobe manager	**Penny Latter**
Production electrician	**Rachel Bowen**
Associate sound designer	**Sean Ephgrave**

If we allow this to continue, we could end up... living in a New Orleans-style Britain of passively co-existing ethnic and religious communities… We are sleepwalking our way to segregation. We are becoming strangers to each other.

Trevor Phillips (Commission for Racial Equality)
September 2005

We have not been sleepwalking into segregation by race, but towards ever greater segregation by wealth and poverty. That matters most to the life chances of people in Britain.

Danny Dorling (University of Sheffield)
The Observer, 25 September 2005

out of joint

"You expect something special from Out of Joint" The Times

Out of Joint is a national and international touring theatre company dedicated to the development and production of new writing. Under the direction of Max Stafford-Clark the company has premiered plays from leading writers including David Hare, Caryl Churchill, Alistair Beaton, Sebastian Barry and Timberlake Wertenbaker, as well as introducing first-time writers such as Simon Bennett, Stella Feehily and Mark Ravenhill.

"Max Stafford-Clark's excellent Out of Joint company" The Independent

Touring all over the UK, Out of Joint frequently performs at and co-produces with key venues such as the Royal Court and the National Theatre. The company has performed in six continents – most recently a world tour of its Africa-inspired *Macbeth*. Back home, Out of Joint also pursues an extensive education programme.

"Out of Joint is out of this world" Boston Globe

Out of Joint's next project is a co-production with Sydney Theatre Company, **The Convict's Opera** - an adaptation of John Gay's *The Beggar's Opera* by Stephen Jeffreys.

Director	**Max Stafford-Clark**
Producer	**Graham Cowley**
Marketing Manager	**Jon Bradfield**
Administrator & Education Manager	**Rebecca Pilbeam**
Assistant Director	**Naomi Jones**
Literary Manager	**Alex Yates**
Finance Officer	**Sandra Palumbo**
PA & Office Assistant	**Maeve McKeown**
TMA Fast Track Intern (until Jan 08)	**Ann Cross**

Board of Directors Kate Ashfield, Linda Bassett, John Blackmore (Chair), Elyse Dodgson, Sonia Friedman, Stephen Jeffreys, Paul Jesson, Danny Sapani, Karl Sydow

Out of Joint
Post: 7 Thane Works, Thane Villas, London N7 7NU
Tel: 020 7609 0207   Fax: 020 7609 0203
Email: ojo@outofjoint.co.uk   Web: www.outofjoint.co.uk

ARTS COUNCIL ENGLAND

KEEP IN TOUCH For information on our shows, tour details and offers, get in touch (contact details above) letting us know whether you'd like to receive information by post or email.

BOOKSHOP Scripts of many of our previous shows are available at exclusive discounted prices from our online shop: www.outofjoint.co.uk

EDUCATION Out of Joint offers a diverse programme of workshops and discussions for groups coming to see our performances. For full details of our education programme, resource packs or Our Country's Good workshops, contact Rebecca at Out of Joint.

Out of Joint is grateful to the following for their support over the years: Arts Council England, The Foundation for Sport and the Arts, The Baring Foundation, The Paul Hamlyn Foundation, The Olivier Foundation, The Peggy Ramsay Foundation, The John S Cohen Foundation, The David Cohen Charitable Trust, The National Lottery through the Arts Council of England, The Prudential Awards, Stephen Evans, Karl Sydow, Harold Stokes and Friends of Theatre, John Lewis Partnership, Royal Victoria Hall Foundation. Out of Joint is a Registered Charity No. 1033059

Top: Teresa Banham; Ian Dunn & Sirine Saba
Centre: Robert Gwilym & Sirine Saba;
Syrus Lowe
Bottom: Kirsty Bushell, Sushil Chudasama &
Farzana Dua Elahe
Over: Matthew Dunster; Robert Gwilym,
Danni Bastian, Naomi Jones, Sirine Saba

TERESA BANHAM

Teresa's **theatre** includes *Heartbreak House* (Watford Palace Theatre); *The Father* (Chichester Festival); *Thomas More, A New Way to Please, Believe What You Will, Speaking Like Magpies* (RSC); *The IO Passion* (Almeida); *One Minute* (The Bush); *Othello* (Northampton/Greenwich); *The Shawl* (Sheffield Crucible); *My Best Friend* (Hampstead Theatre); *Snake in the Grass* (Old Vic); *The Herbal Bed, The White Devil, Blue Angel, Measure for Measure* (RSC/Young Vic); *Anna Karenina* (Shared Experience); *Here* (Donmar Warehouse); *Valentine's Day* (Gielgud). **Television** includes *Dalziel & Pascoe, Trial and Retribution, Vincent, Rose and Maloney, Redcaps, Trust, The Project, Gentleman's Relish, Monsignor Renard, Touch and Go, Out of Hours, The Six Sides of Steve Coogan, Roughnecks, Massage* (Ghost Hour), *The Healer, The Bill, Reasonable Force, After the War, Cariani and the Courtesan, The Adventures of Sherlock Holmes.*

KIRSTY BUSHELL

Kirsty appeared in the world tour of Out of Joint's *Blue Heart*. Other **theatre** includes a TMA award-nominated performance in *Angels In America* (Headlong/Glasgow Citizens Theatre/Lyric Hammersmith); *Twelfth Night* (Filter/RSC); *The Voysey Inheritance* (National Theatre); *Comedy of Errors, Girl in the Goldfish Bowl, Fen/Far Away* (Sheffield Crucible); *Don Juan* (Lyric Hammersmith); *Mere Mortals* (Sure Thing Productions); *The Seagull* (Northampton Theatre); *An Inspector Calls* (National Theatre/Garrick); *The Importance of Being Earnest* (Newbury Watermill); *Macbeth, BFG* (Nuffield Theatre); *The Suppliants* (Gate); *The Two Gentlemen of Verona* (National Theatre Education). **Television** includes *Pulling, Eastenders, Midsomer Murders, Talk to Me, Holby City, The Bill, Family Man, Life Isn't All Ha Ha Hee Hee, Roger Roger.* **Film**: *Really.*

SUSHIL CHUDASAMA

Sushil's **theatre** includes the New Writing Festival at Oldham Coliseum; *The Kindness of Strangers,* (Everyman Liverpool); *Toba Tek Singh* (Gateway Theatre Edinburgh); *Flip the Script* (LeKoa); *Krindlekrax* (Birmingham Rep/Nottingham Playhouse); *Mapping the Edge* (Wilson Wilson Co.) *Queuing for Everest* (Crucible, Sheffield); *Choice, East Meets West* (Royal Court). **Television** includes *Waterloo Road, Drop Dead Gorgeous, Coronation Street, Northern Exposure, Blue Murder II, Clocking Off III & IV, Casualty, A+E, Off Side, Strumpet, Doctors, Belonging, The Cops, Shipman, Cold Feet* and *The Dream Team.* He appeared in the **film** *Chicken Tikka Masala.* **Radio** includes *Silver Street* (series) and *A Minus.*

New Welsh accents could emerge as a result of recent migration from Eastern Europe… David Crystal, a professor from Anglesey, said foreign accents could quickly begin to influence the way indigenous youngsters spoke. He warned that older people in some communities could be unsettled as accents changed… "As soon as you get a reasonable-sized community… you get a distinctive local accent emerging… Some people might make fun of it but other people – youngsters – might find it a bit cool to copy them, as with hip hop in London….If you're a Polish kid, you're going to share the same music interests as the Welsh kids do.

Rhodri Clark, Western Mail, 30 April 2007

IAN DICKINSON *Sound Designer*

Ian designed the sound for Out of Joint and Hampstead Theatre's *King of Hearts*. For the Royal Court: *The Family Plays*, *Rhinoceros*, *My Child*, *The Eleventh Capital*, *The Seagull*, *Krapp's Last Tape*, *Piano/Forte*, *Rock 'n' Roll* (& Duke of York's & Broadway), *Motortown*, *Rainbow Kiss*, *The Winterling*, *Alice Trilogy*, *Fewer Emergencies*, *Way to Heaven*, *The Woman Before*, *Stoning Mary* (& Drum Theatre, Plymouth), *Breathing Corpses*, *Wild East*, *Dumb Show*, *Shining City* (& The Gate, Dublin), *Lucky Dog*, *Blest Be the Tie* (with Talawa), *Ladybird*, *Notes on Falling Leaves*, *Loyal Women*, *The Sugar Syndrome*, *Blood*, *Playing the Victim* (with Told By an Idiot), *Fallout*, *Flesh Wound*, *Hitchcock Blonde* (& Lyric), *Black Milk*, *Crazyblackmuthafuckin'self*, *Caryl Churchill Shorts*, *Push Up*, *Fucking Games*, *Herons*. Other theatre includes: *Love and Money* (Young Vic); *Much Ado About Nothing* (redesign, RSC/Novello); *The Hothouse*, *Pillars of the Community* (National Theatre); *A Few Good Men* (Haymarket); *Dr Faustus* (Chichester Festival Theatre); *The Magic Carpet* (Lyric Hammersmith); *Port*, *As You Like It*, *Poor Superman*, *Martin Yesterday*, *Fast Food*, *Coyote Ugly* (Royal Exchange, Manchester); *Night of the Soul* (RSC/Barbican); *Under the Curse*, *Eyes of the Kappa* (Gate); *Crime & Punishment in Dalston* (Arcola); *Search & Destroy* (New End); *The Whore's Dream* (RSC/Edinburgh). Ian is Head of Sound at the Royal Court.

FARZANA DUA ELAHE

Farzana's theatre appearances include *Catch* (Royal Court); *Burn & Citizenship* (National Theatre);*The Pilgrimage* (Young Vic); *Family Ties* (Greenwich Theatre); *Fresh Start* (Round House Space); *Dust* (Albany Theatre). **Television** credits include *Omid*, *Britz*, *Spit Game*, *Doctors*, *M.I.T.*, *England Expects*, *The Bill*. **Film** includes *Saxon*.

IAN DUNN

Ian's **theatre** includes : *Cruising* (Bush Theatre), *Osama The Hero*, *A Single Act* (Hampstead Theatre); *Project C: On Principle* (Battersea Arts Centre); *A Doll's House* (Southwark Playhouse);*Terrorism*, *Fucking Games*, *Toast*, *I Am Yours*, *Babies* (Royal Court); *Luminosity*, *Love Play* (RSC); *Chips With Everything*, *Somewhere* (National Theatre); *Our Boys* (Donmar Warehouse/Derby Playhouse); *Six Degrees of Separation* (Royal Court/Comedy Theatre); *A Prayer for Wings* (Tour); *Hidden Laughter* (Vaudeville); *Forget-Me-Not Lane* (Greenwich); *Invisible Friends*, *Wolf at the Door*, *Brighton Beach Memoirs* (Stephen Joseph Theatre, Scarborough). **Television** includes *Waking the Dead*, *Holby City*, *Heartbeat*, *Silent Witness*, *Pulling*, *French & Saunders*, *Holby City*, *Doctors*, *Murphy's Law*, *Sea Of Souls*, *Red Cap*, *Girls In Love* (series 1&2), *Trust*, *London's Burning*, *Peak Practice*, *Bad Girls*, *Holby City*, *The Bill*, *Reach For The Moon*, *Bliss*, *Stone*, *Scissors & Paper*, *Gulliver's Travel*, *Shine On Harvey Moon*, *Casualty*, *Desmonds*, *Jackanory*: *The Gulf*, *The Merrihill Millionaires*, *A Touch Of Frost*, *Soldier Soldier*, *Children of The North*, *Sweet Capital Lives*. **Films** include *American Friends* and *Bye Bye Baby*. He has also been in numerous **radio** productions.

MATTHEW DUNSTER *Director*

Matthew is an Associate Director of The Young Vic where he has directed *The Member of the Wedding*, the Olivier-nominated *Love and Money* (also Royal Exchange, Manchester) and *Some Voices*. Other directing work includes *Cruising* (Bush); *Project D: I'm Mediocre* (The Work) and *Port Authority* (Liverpool Everyman). Writing for the stage includes *You Used To Tell Me*, *Two Clouds Over Eden* and the forthcoming *You Can See The Hills* (Royal Exchange Manchester). Writing for radio includes: *Depth of Field* (winner Best Radio Drama Mental Health In Media Awards) and *Poor Echo*. As an actor Matthew appeared in Out of Joint and the National Theatre's *The Permanent Way*. Other theatre includes *Toast*, *Plasticine*, *Under The Whaleback*, *Harvest* (Royal Court); and *The Daughter-in-Law* (Young Vic). Many television appearances include a spell in *Coronation Street*.

It is an offence for someone to harrass you or for you to harrass another person because of their nationality, religion, ethnic origin or colour. It is also an offence for your partner to be violent towards you or for you to be violent towards them. It is also a criminal offence to force a woman to have sex with you if she says no. You must be over 16 to purchase cigarettes and over 18 to purchase alcohol... Possession or the intention to supply, or supplying certain drugs is illegal and a criminal offence. Having sex with a minor... or a member of your family is also a criminal offence.

No. 8, from *Ten Things you Need to Know*
- A Welcome to Wales Pack for Migrant Workers. Welsh Assembly Government.

DAVID EDGAR *Writer*

David's **plays** include *Destiny* (Royal Shakespeare Company, 1976, winner of the John Whiting Award), *Maydays* (RSC 1983, Plays and Players Play of the Year Award), *That Summer* (Hampstead Theatre, London, 1987), and *Playing with Fire* (National Theatre, 2005). He wrote a series of plays about Eastern Europe after the Cold War: *The Shape of the Table* (NT 1990), *Pentecost* (RSC 1994, Evening Standard Best Play Award) and *The Prisoner's Dilemma* (RSC 2001). His **stage adaptations** include *Jail Diary* (RSC, 1978), *Mary Barnes* (Birmingham Rep/Royal Court 1978-9), an award-winning version of *Nicholas Nickleby* (RSC, 1980, recently revived by the Chichester Festival Theatre, on tour and in London); *Dr Jekyll and Mr Hyde* (RSC 1991) and *Albert Speer* (NT, 2000). He has written two **community plays** for Dorchester: *Entertaining Strangers* (1985, later produced at the National) and *A Time to Keep* (2007, written with Stephanie Dale). **Television** work includes *Buying a Landslide* (BBC2) and *Citizen Locke* (Channel Four). **Radio** plays include *Talking to Mars*, *Something wrong about the mouth*, an adaptation of *Playing with Fire* and an adaptation of Eve Brook's novel *The Secret Parts*. Edgar founded Britain's first post-graduate course in playwriting, at the University of Birmingham, and is a frequent broadcaster, commentator and reviewer for the BBC, the Guardian, the London Review of Books and other journals. He is President of the Writers' Guild.

PHILIP GLADWELL *Lighting Designer*

Most recently Philip has lit: *Terminus* at The Public Theatre New York; *Anansi Trades Places* for Talawa Theatre Co. *Crestfall* at Theatre 503. Other **theatre** includes: *Kebab* (Royal Court); *The Member of the Wedding*, *Winners*, *Interior*, *The Exception and the Rule*, *The New Tennant*, *When The World Was Green*, *The Soul of Ch'ien Nu Leaves Her Body* (Young Vic); *Melody*, *In The Bag* (Traverse); *Midnight Cowboy* (Assembly); *A Whistle in the Dark* (Citizens); *HOTBOI*, *Tape* (Soho Theatre); *Jack and the Beanstalk*, *Aladdin* (Hackney Empire); *Dead Funny*, *Mother Courage* (Nottingham Playhouse & UK tour); *Into The Woods*, *Macbeth*, *Way up Stream* (Derby Playhouse); *The Bodies* (Live Theatre); *The Morris* (Liverpool Everyman); *Bread & Butter* (Tricycle); *I'm Mediocre* (The Work); *Mixed Feelings* (UK tour); *Sophie Tucker's One Night Stand* (Kings Head); *Paper Thin* (Kali theatre Co. tour); *Dreams From a Summer House* (Watermill); *Modern Love* (Queen Elizabeth Hall). **Opera & Ballet** include *Il Trittico* (Opera Zuid); *Cavalleria Rusticana & Pagliacci* (Haddo House Opera); *An Operatic Evening* (Royal Opera House); *Another America: Fire* (Sadlers Wells); *The Canterville Ghost* (Peacock); *Awakening* (Sadlers Wells).

ROBERT GWILYM

Robert's recent **theatre** includes *Antigone*, *Aladdin*, and the title role in *Macbeth* (Bristol Old Vic). Other theatre includes: *A View from the Bridge* (Touring Consortium); *Cymbeline*, *Pericles*, *Baal*, *The Suicide* (RSC); *The Seagull*, *The White Devil*, *The Way of the World* (Greenwich); *Behind Heaven* (Manchester Royal Exchange/Donmar Warehouse); *Sgt Musgrave's Dance* (Oxford Playhouse); *Under Milk Wood*, *Entertaining Mr Sloane* (Thorndyke); *Much Ado About Nothing*, *Ivanov* (Strand); *Dancing at Lughnasa* (Abbey Theatre, Dublin/West End/Broadway); *Wintershall Passion Play*, *Julius Caesar* (Exchange); *The Mai* (Tricycle); *Othello* (Nottingham Playhouse) and over 25 productions at The Citizen's Theatre, Glasgow. **Television** includes: *The Bill*, *Forty Something*, *Ultimate Force*, *Casualty*, *Taggart*, *Tiger Bay*, *Chef*, *Soldier Soldier*, *Macgyver*, *Unexplained Laughter*, *Lovejoy*, *The Devil's Crown*, *Much Ado About Nothing*, *Operation Julie*, *The Brothers Karamazov*, *Ballroom*, *The Zero Option*, *South of the Border* and *The Professionals*. **Film** includes: *Mussolini*, *Sakharov*, *On the Black Hill*. **Radio** includes: *Sense and Sensibility*, *Guards! Guards!*, *The Fantasy of Dr Ox*, *Quantum Man*, *Three Days that Shook the World*, *Delayed Departures*, *A City Full of Swindlers*.

SALLY HAGUE *Dialect Coach*

Sally is a graduate of the Voice Studies course at Central School of Speech and Drama. She teaches at RADA. Her many theatre credits include; *Rat Pack Confidential* (Whitehall Theatre); *Sugar Mommies* (Royal Court); *Boeing Boeing*, (Comedy Theatre); *Rent* (Duke of Yorks); *The Member of the Wedding* (Young Vic);

...**a schedule of** "non-negotiable" value statements to which every citizen is expected to sign up is not in the spirit of an open, plural citizenship. National identity should be woven in debate and discussion, not reduced to a list. For central to it is a citizenship and the right of all, especially previously marginalised or newly admitted groups, to make a claim on the national identity... Being black or Muslim is then no longer seen as something to be tolerated but part of what it is to be British today.

Tariq Mamood, The Guardian, 23 May 2007

Day's Journey into Night (Druid Theatre Galway); *The Grapes of Wrath* and *Mice and Men* (Theatre
d, Mold).

MI JONES *Assistant Director*

mi recently directed *Flight Path* for Out of Joint; *Machinal* (Oxford School of Drama at BAC); *One Million
Plays About London* (Clerkenwell Theatre); and *After Miss Julie* (GEST, Sweden); as well as the revival
ssell Barr's hit *Sisters, Such Devoted Sisters* (Drill Hall). As Assistant Director at Out of Joint Naomi has
ed on *Duck, The Permanent Way, Macbeth, Talking to Terrorists, O go my Man* and *King of Hearts.*

JS LOWE

s graduated from RADA in 2007. Just after graduating he was part of the Old Vic's *The Sky's The Limit*
ct and then began filming an eight episode special for *The Bill* (January 2008). *Testing The Echo* is
s's professional stage debut.

NE SABA

e's **theatre** credits include *Baghdad Wedding* (Soho Theatre); *The Taming of the Shrew, A Midsummer
ts Dream, Twelfth Night, HMS Pinafore* (Regents Park Open Air Theatre); *Beauty and The Beast, Midnight's
dren, The Tempest, Pericles, The Winter's Tale, A Warwickshire Testimony, Tales from Ovid, A Midsummer
t's Dream* (RSC); *Soho* (RSC Fringe); *Cinderella* (Bristol Old Vic); *Our Town, The Pillars of Society* (RNT
io); *House & Garden* (Northampton); *Sparkleshark* (National Theatre); *The King and I* (BAC); *Paper
and* (Rosemary Branch). **Television & Film** include *Silent Witness, Footballers Wives Extra Time, Death of
Revolution, The Bill, Do's and Don'ts, Prometheus.* **Radio** includes *Love and Loss* and *Baghdad Wedding.*

L WILLS *Designer*

is also designing *The Man Who Had All The Luck* (Donmar Warehouse). Other theatre credits include
tfall* (Theatre 503); *We The People* (Globe); *The Changeling, Mother Courage* (both set design, ETT); *Tracy
ker Gets Real* (Nottingham and Tour); *Prometheus Bound* (New York and The Sound Venue); *Sleeping
uty* (Helix, Dublin); *The Cut* (Donmar & Tour); *Little Voice* (Watermill); *Total Eclipse* (Menier Chocolate
ory); *A Model Girl* (Greenwich); *The Field* (Tricycle); *Invisible Mountains* (NT Education Tour); *Mammals
h & Tour); *Breathing Corpses* (Royal Court); a Pinter triple bill - *A Kind of Alaska, A Slight Ache* and
isely* (Gate); *A Number* (Sheffield Crucible & Chichester); *Gladiator Games* (Sheffield Crucible & Stratford
; *Blue/Orange, Batina and the Moon* (Sheffield Crucible); *A Streetcar Named Desire* (Clwyd); *Oliver!
eford); *A Thousand Yards* (Southwark Playhouse); *References to Salvador Dali Make Me Hot* (Arcola); *Car
ves* (Birmingham Rep); *The School of Night* (The Other Place). He also designed *Sweetness and Badness*
Welsh National Opera's Max project and *The Magic Flute* for The National Theatre of Palestine.

cenery Construction by Robert Knight Scenery
ighting Equipment: Stage Electrics ; Video Equipment: XL Video
ound Equipment: Cue One
Vith thanks to: The Young Vic, Stuart Milligan and Phil Bradley

ree **EDUCATION WORKPACK is available to download from www.outofjoint.co.uk**

we put our desire to defend the right to be different ahead of our fight for
e right to be equal we can end up by excluding and diminishing the most
advantaged people in our society.

vor Phillips, 26 April 2004

DEFINING A NATION
Bernard Crick on two senses of citizenship

When Labour came to power in 1997 many advisory committees were set up. So
were PR gestures, perhaps never meant to report in time or, if so, were kicked i
touch. A big exception was citizenship.

The new Secretary of State for Education, David Blunkett, had long be
passionate to increase popular involvement in politics and knew that schools w
the starting point. Before he became Blairite he was something of a communitari
Despite worries in No 10 that it would be political dynamite, he set up a stro
committee, asked me to chair it (way back in 1978 I had been instigator and ch
of a Hansard Society report, *Political Education and Political Literacy*). Its remit w
"To provide advice on effective education for citizenship in schools—to inclu
the nature and practices of participation in democracy; the duties, responsibilit
and rights of individuals as citizens; and the values to individuals and society
community activity".

"Participation" was the term we seized on – "active citizenship" not j
passive "good citizenship". And Blunkett urged that it should be a "light tou
curriculum, leaving an unusual amount of discretion to teachers - in contradict
to the rest of the national curriculum.

Instead of the old leadership ethic of the public schools we wante
participative ethic in state schools. The report took the radical stand that desp
our long and once-upon-a-time much envied parliamentary tradition, there h
developed what is now often called "a democratic deficit" in society as a whole.
a changing society we have been living on the top-down political traditions of t
past. Young people had become cynical of politics – or was it of politicians? -- a
voting turnout was falling especially among the under-25s. The aim of adding a n
subject to the relatively new national curriculum was to create a general "politi
literacy: "an active and politically- literate citizenry convinced that they can influer
government and community affairs at all levels".

"Political literacy" was a term invented to mean that someone should ha
the knowledge, skills and values to be effective in public life. Citizenship is not j
individuals knowing their rights: it is people acting together for a common purpo
The report had an implied methodology for teaching and learning: that knowled
of institutions is best gained through lively discussion of real and contentio
issues. Then people will want to know what institutions are relevant and need
to influence or resolve an issue or problem. Teaching about institutions and le

We won the Olympic bid by making a promise to the world that, in London, we h
a vision of ourselves as united by pride in our diversity and a commitment to t
idea that, whatever our backgrounds, we all deserve the opportunity to fulfil o
potential. While this might not be an entirely accurate picture of today's London
Britain, much work has been put into trying to achieve this goal: we have the be
race relations and religious discrimination laws in Europe, and are moving in t
right direcron.

Sadiq Khan, Is Britishness relevant?
From "Britishness: Towards a progressive citizenship", published by the Smith Institute (200

wers on their own is, if easily examinable, dead boring – old fashioned "Civics".

Still not all teachers grasp this. Four years into the new subject, about a rd of schools still nervously shelter behind old Civics, but a third have leapt at it: nore participative school can enthuse all subjects. Another third do well enough itizenship lessons but do little to affect the culture of the school.

This led on to my involvement with The 1998 Immigration and turalisation Act which demanded that people should have "sufficient" knowledge English language and British institutions. I had no difficulty with that: I am all multiculturalism; but that means integration and mutual understanding not rpetuating segregation. Given wide discretion to find and recommend the visory group, I ended up with fifty-fifty old Brits and new Brits and fifty-fifty men d women. I'm not very PC. That's just how it was. Women predominate both in guage teaching and social work (and women immigrants need the most help). I nt for people with hands-on experience not "names".

Despite sniping and mockery in the popular press, ministers accepted our pposals that citizenship could be granted for certified progress at quite low levels in professional language classes with citizenship content (ESOL classes); or, if applicants think their English good enough, a machine-readable test (like the driving test) based on sections of a handbook we had compiled, *Life in the United Kingdom: a journey to citizenship* (now the Stationery Office's best-seller). The BBC called it "the Britishness test". No such thing, it was a test of information useful for settling in Britain. Newspapers asked their readers model history tests and nearly all seemed designed to stop people becoming izens (you all know the date of *Magna Carta*, don't you?).

ewspapers asked eir readers to come p with tests - nearly l seemed designed stop people ecoming citizens

By all means discuss "what is Britishness" both in school and in ESOL classes, t any attempt to define it precisely in a curriculum is both fatuous and oppressive. y group took the view that living in Britain, understanding our customs and being ated decently, constitutes Britishness. But Blair and Blunkett seemed to favour ting on history. So a last-minute compromise was reached. I wrote (in a hurry) an torical introduction to the handbook, but as background information, not for the t (now corrected and toned down under civil service eyes).

My group saw the new regulations for citizenship as an entitlement and incentive; indeed the citizenship ceremonies have proved very popular. But ere has been insufficient funding, and increased fees; and now ministers are too

e **Olympics is** but one example of a national project which is uniting the untry

rdon Brown, 14 January 2006

nervous of the anti-immigration press to claim credit for encouraging naturalisat
there is the threat that the new system becomes a deterrent. Now that the P
have answered the shortage of labour, third-world immigration is only for the v
highly skilled. (Des Browne, when Minister for Immigration, was angry with me
remarking that Downing Street must have realised that there were no Black Pol

And the test without the preliminary citizenship classes we
recommended is in danger of degenerating – as I blurted out on the To
programme – into a pub quiz.

Bernard Crick is author of *In Defence of Politics*, *George Orwell: a life* and *Essays on Citizensh*

HARDWIRED FOR GLOBALISATION
Abdul-Rehman Malik on becoming a Brit

I migrated to Britain in 2003 because of love. My London-born wife grew
abroad and returned to her birthplace in 2001, eager to live out the promise
her citizenship after a lifetime in the arid confines of Singapore. We met throu
Q-News, the British Muslim magazine she now edits and with which I had be
involved since 1995.

Britain was not unfamiliar to me. My father spent several heady ye
here in the 1960s, studying and being a Mus
hippie, before settling in Canada. I spent m
of my university holidays between London a
Liverpool (where my aunt lived). London v
the kind of city I wanted Toronto to be – vibra
bewildering, pregnant with possibility. I loved
"We are The World" look of Home Office officials
the border – a mix of hijabs, turbans, accents a
complexions.

British Muslims seemed exciting, asking questions like whether there was more to being a Muslim than beards

Being born in 1970s Canada meant being born with an ident
crisis. Quebec had a vibrant, and sometimes violent, separatist moveme
Immigrants, mostly skilled and in high demand (like my parents who came fro
Pakistan), were changing the fabric of our urban centres. Aboriginal peopl
"Indians", struggled to find a voice at the table of public policy after decades
neglect and, sometimes, abuse had left their communities in near "third wor

Take the colony as it stands. Eliminate the idea that it represents an invasion a
treat its members neither as foreigners nor as paupers. Look at them as citize
ratepayers, heads of families and trades people. Inquire how far they fulfil t
ordinary duties of civilised life as members of a free and independent commun
The answer to that question might be given in a single sentence: they never forc
they are Jews and that other people are gentiles. They are a people apart. Long
they may live among us they will never become merged in the mass of the Engl
population.

Article in the St James Gazette, 1887

...ing the Echo in rehearsal

conditions. To accommodate the desire of the Quebecois to be recognised as unique and distinct, Canada was an officially bilingual nation. French was taught to us from primary school. Accommodating the rest of us, however, wasn't going to be as easy. In defining what being a Canadian means it has always been easier to say what we are not, rather than what we are. And above all, we are not American. Emphatically. Not. American.

To a Canadian Muslim ...ivist, British Muslims seemed edgy, exciting. The people at Q-News, who so ...uenced my intellectual development, were asking questions like whether ...ere was more to being Muslim than "beards, scarves and halal meat" and ...sing the red flag on the inevitable cruelty of extreme religion when it was ...fashionable to do so. I resolved to one day find an excuse to live here. The ...cuse found me.

Perhaps because my Canadian passport gives me certain unearned ...vileges, acquiring a spouse settlement visa and then an "indefinite leave to ...main" was an easy process. When I called the official hotlines my queries were ...swered without judgement and when I accidentally neglected to renew my ...tlement visa in time, a plaintive letter explaining my circumstances did the ...ck.

The requirements for British citizenship are straightforward: possess an ...definite leave to remain", be resident for a required number of years without ...y recourse to public funds, pay income tax, be clear of a criminal record, be ..."good character" and of "sound mind" (one would think this would disqualify ...any born Britons) and successfully complete the citizenship test.

The "Life in the UK" test is the way in which prospective citizens are

Blair's decade, people not of the British tribe have settled in these islands... ...ome] will neither integrate nor go away. They will stay here - separate, resentful, ...nging to turn the country into one more like the one they have left, living separate ...es in cultural and linguistic ghettos... The tribe is being broken up: its history ...taught, values brought into contempt, institutions defiled, solidarity dissolved ...the corrosive mixture of continental law, political correctness and the avarice, ...rruption and celebrity culture of its political and social elite.

...rman Tebbit, The Guardian, 4 May 2007

asked to demonstrate their understanding of what it means to be a Brit
citizen. If you can cram for exams, read basic English and navigate a mil
complicated computer program, you should do fine. These seem rather we
qualifications to judge whether one is suitable prepared to take on the ro
and responsibilities of citizenship, but such emphasis is placed on the test th
the experience is deeply nerve-wracking. I put it off until my wife booke(
date and said I had to show up or else. For a week, I read and re-read "Life in t
UK – A Journey to Citizenship" and even paid two entrepreneurial websites
supply me with sample tests. I learned about the Patron Saints, the year wom
gained suffrage and the percentage of the population that is considered "your
– information that many who are born Britons would struggle to remember.

At the test centre, we study-weary prospective citizens – Canadian
noticed familiar accents), Poles, Bangladeshis, Iranians, Kurds, Chinese and a v(
loud American - sit waiting to be called to the computers. We have 45 minu
to complete 24 multiple-choice questions. I finish in 3 minutes 27 seconds a
am soon handed a certificate confirming that I passed. As I walk out, I notic(
middle-aged Kurdish couple sitting in the waiting area. The woman dabs I
eyes with a tissue - she hasn't passed.

I am now on the cusp of officially becoming a British citizen. F
over four years, I have immersed myself in British life – from the classroo
at the London School of Economics to studios at the BBC to commun
organising - engaging wholeheartedly in the discussion about what it me(
to live in a multicultural society. I have tried to behave as if I already belong(
Nevertheless, my accent and my failure, from time to time, to get pop cultu
references ("What's Dad's Army got to do with this anyways?") betray my migra
status. After a public debate on being "Young, British and Muslim", a group
young Muslims challenged my take on the "Muslim situation". One finally sai(
exasperation, "Look mate, you haven't even got our accent! You're never rea
gonna be British!" Patriotism is still the last refuge of the scoundrel.

With my "indefinite leave to remain" permit, I can own property, work and v(
in the UK without becoming a citizen. I can even work as a civil servant, G(
forbid. It's not enough for me. Citizenship means making a conscious decisi(
to be invested in the country I now call home – it may be one of many hom(
but it is without a doubt home. It also means easy passage to the EU, few
question at Heathrow and lower fees if I finally do my PhD.

The national 'we' is always in some ways a fiction and 'us' and 'the
distinctions are a normal component of national life. Such a view is n
necessarily inimical to the craving for oneness. As the Conservati
philosopher Edmund Burke put it: it is by our attachment to the 'litt
platoons' that we become members of the great society.

Raphael Samuel, Patriotism Vol II, 1989

What does it mean to be British? It's a question most Britons would ve difficulty answering. It's a question that fascinates me. The experience of ng British is different from the corridors of a council estate than it is from a : in Mayfair. A country forged from the union of four "nations" has identity sis woven into the very fabric of its existence.

I don't have to renounce my Canadian citizenship. Other new Britons e not so lucky. Their loyalties are persistently questioned: Muslim or British? kistani or English? As if we cannot be both (or more) at the same time. Our perience of migration, the collective memory of colonisation, the lived lity of the click that takes us from Tower Hamlets to Toronto to Timbuktu nanoseconds does not easily fit in with the kind of flag-waving that policy kers are eager to promote.

I belong to a generation that is hardwired for globalisation. I am a smopolitan by birth, the son of a migrant who was the son of a migrant who s the son of a migrant. Leaving and arriving are the threads that hold my ry together.

Young Muslims, in particular, are turned on to the global village. these global souls, discrete national identity seems like a straightjacket. ndon, on the other hand, fits the global soul like a second skin. It anonymises at the same time as accepting us. I can feel passionate about London – great ies inspire visions of great societies. Nation states are unwieldy, cities are al. As social researcher Steve Vertovec points out, many young Muslims feel ong affinity to their locales – Bradford, Birmingham, London – and strong nnection to global notions of community, like the *ummah*. National identities e often not compelling enough.

In the handwringing over national values, we forget that nations and tionalisms are not static. Values are best developed as a result of vigorous bate, not social engineering. I believe that Britain is, and always will be a work progress. The reality of "Middle England" is not my reality and is increasingly noved from the reality of Britain 2.0. Britain is formed and re-formed every y by her citizens. It seems we "newcomers" have embraced the mongrel aracter of this English race.

dul-Rehman Malik is a journalist and contributing editor with Q-News he Muslim Magazine.

ecent debates on integration and identity have problematised Muslim ess, lifestyle, culture, organisations and our place in society itself. This has d to Muslims feeling beleaguered, misunderstood and weary of constantly ercoming stereotypes.

ma Yaqoob, Comment is free… Guardian Blog, 4 July 2007

BBC Radio 4's *Today* programme invited a panel of guests to draw up 10 questio
any British citizen should be able to answer. Compiling the questions were: Barr
Beerman MP; the historian Andrew Roberts; Trevor Phillips (then the deputy
chairman of the Greater London Assembly); Zara Joseph of the British Muslim
Council; and economist Madsen Pirie.

Answers below. (With kind permission of the BBC)

1) Which king had his powers curbed by the Magna Carta?
    a) Alfred b) Charles I c) John

2) Which date did all women over 21 get the vote in Britain?
    a) 1945 b) 1900 c) 1928

3) Which three branches of the authority need to agree to a law before it can come into force?
    a) The House of Commons, Lord Chancellor and the Queen
    b) The House of Commons, the Lords and the Queen
    c) The Prime Minister the Cabinet and the police.

4) Are you a…
    a) Subject of the Crown
    b) Citizen of the Crown
    c) Defender of the Crown

5) Why is the Union Jack made up of its particular colours?
    a) It was chosen by Henry VIII,
    b) It's made up of the flags of St George of England, St Patrick of Ireland and St Andrew of Scotland
    c) It's made of the flags of England and the flags of the Anglo-Saxon Kingdoms of Mercia and Wessex.

6) Is a man allowed to punish his wife physically as long as it's in his own home?
    a) Yes, although not with any recognised weapon
    b) Yes, although only under provocation
    c) No

7) Which English monarch broke away from the Roman Catholic Church?
    a) Charles I b) Elizabeth I c) Henry V

8) Who was the only politician in Briti history to abolish parliament?
    a) Cromwell b) Gladstone c) Churc

9) What did Guy Fawkes famously fail to do?
    a) Blow up Buckingham Palace
    b) Blow up the Houses of Parliamen
    c) Blow up 10 Downing St

10) How long can a British governme stay in office before a general electio
    a) 4 yrs b) 6 yrs c) 5 yrs

ANSWERS: 1) c) John. 2) c) 1928
3) b) Commons, Lords & the Queen 4) a) Subject
5) b) St George of England, St Patrick of Ireland and
Andrew of Scotland 6) c) No 7) c) Henry VIII
8) a) Cromwell 9) b) Houses of Parliament
10) c) 5 yrs **…but what questions would you ask?**

TESTING THE ECHO

David Edgar

To Max

Characters

JAMAL
MAHMOOD
BERNIE

ASSISTANT REGISTRAR
MAYOR

EMMA
SAMIR
HALIMA
RANJIT
JASMINKA
DRAGOSLAV
BABA
NASIM
TOBY

CHONG
DEREK
JOSHUA
CHLOE

TETYANA
AZIZ
WEBSITE
MUNA

1ST HISTORIAN
2ND HISTORIAN
3RD HISTORIAN
1ST EDITION
2ND EDITION
1ST CIVIL SERVANT
2ND CIVIL SERVANT
MINISTER

PAULINE
MARTIN
IAN

NEW CITIZENS,
    BLOGGERS, *etc*.

*This text went to press before the end of rehearsals and so may
differ slightly from the play as performed.*

Doubling

The play is written for eight actors, four men and four women.

Where the actors speak as themselves, I have attributed the lines to the original actors (Teresa, Kirsty, Sushil, Farzana, Ian, Robert, Syrus and Sirine). For the named parts, the doubling structure for the original production was:

Emma/Bernie
Tetyana/Pauline/Halima
Mahmood/Ian/Dragoslav
Muna/Jasminka
Chong/Aziz/Samir/Toby
Mayor/Derek/Martin/Ranjit
Jamal/Joshua/Baba
Assistant Registrar/Chloe/Nasim

Notation and languages

A dash (–) means that a character is interrupted. A slash (/) means that the next character to speak starts speaking at that point (what follows the slash need not be completed, it is there to indicate the character's train of thought). Ellipses (…) indicate that a character has interrupted him or herself. When the characters speak languages other than English, I have identified the languages and given English translations of the non-English speeches (printed in square brackets and obviously not intended to be spoken). When the language is or can be written in Roman script (such as the various languages of the former Yugoslavia) the language is rendered as conventionally written. In languages written in other scripts (such as Arabic and Korean) the dialogue is rendered phonetically. When characters are speaking to themselves or the audience, their names are followed by '2'.

D.E.

Scene One

Top-floor room, West Yorkshire. JAMAL *throws* MAHMOOD *into the room.* MAHMOOD *is blindfolded by a wrong-way balaclava and his hands are tied with duct tape.* JAMAL *shouts at him in Arabic.*

JAMAL (*Arabic*). *Hena hena, escot.* [In here. In here, keep quiet.]

MAHMOOD. Hey, man.

JAMAL (*Arabic*). *Escot la tataharak fe al-ghorfa.* [Keep quiet and don't move about the room.]

MAHMOOD. Man, what's happening?

JAMAL (*Arabic*). *Sawfa-tazal hona hata yantahy alámal.* [This is where you stay until the job's done.]

MAHMOOD. What's going off, for Christ's sake?

JAMAL (*Arabic*). *Haza manzelak al-aan.* [This is your home now.]

MAHMOOD. This is bang out of order, man.

JAMAL (*Arabic*). *Ana aqool lak haza manzelak al-gadeed.* [I tell you, this is your new home.]

MAHMOOD. I dunno what you're fucking saying.

JAMAL (*Arabic*). *Sawfa tamkoth hona hata tantahy.* [This is where you'll be until you're finished.]

MAHMOOD. Where am I?

JAMAL *rips* MAHMOOD's *balaclava off.*

JAMAL. This is your home now.

MAHMOOD. What?

JAMAL. This is where you're stopping.

MAHMOOD. Hey, Jamal.

JAMAL. Chair. Mat.

MAHMOOD. Oh, right. Like the first thing I'm going to do is /
kneel down –

JAMAL. I'll be back later.

MAHMOOD. You can't go.

JAMAL. I'll be back later on.

MAHMOOD. You can't leave me.

JAMAL. I'll be back this evening.

MAHMOOD. Hallo? I've got to eat, man.

JAMAL. I'll bring you takeaway.

MAHMOOD. Takeaway? I can't eat fucking takeaway.

JAMAL. What do you want to eat?

MAHMOOD. I want you to let me out of here.

JAMAL. You want to do this. What do you want to eat?

MAHMOOD. I need tinned soup. Chicken or tomato. Yoghurt.
Smoothies. Paracetamol. I could eat dhal.

JAMAL. OK.

MAHMOOD. Can I see Bernie?

JAMAL. Bernie?

MAHMOOD. Girlfriend.

JAMAL. Of course you can't see your kufr girlfriend.

MAHMOOD. Where the fuck am I?

JAMAL. Of course I can't tell you where you are.

    MAHMOOD *grabs a chair.*

MAHMOOD. OK. I'll throw this through the window. You let
me out of here or I throw this through the window.

JAMAL. They ask us to do this.

MAHMOOD. Eh?

JAMAL. They ask us to do this. 'For his own sake.'

MAHMOOD. Who's 'they'?

JAMAL. I can't tell you.

MAHMOOD. Were it my brother or my auntie?

JAMAL. I can't tell you.

MAHMOOD. You tell me else I throw this through the window.

JAMAL. I can't tell you.

MAHMOOD. You promise to bring my fucking kufr girlfriend, else I throw this through the window.

Pause.

Kids. Kids on the street.

JAMAL. She'd have to be blindfold.

MAHMOOD. Fine.

JAMAL. She don't stay no more than half an hour.

MAHMOOD. Done.

JAMAL. She don't bring you nothing.

MAHMOOD. Done.

JAMAL. She's clean.

MAHMOOD. Done.

JAMAL. And you pray.

MAHMOOD. You what?

JAMAL. You pray now.

MAHMOOD. Pray? Why?

JAMAL. *Why?*

Pause.

Because you are not Maz or Micky now. No more just an echo of shit English person and shit English life.

MAHMOOD *puts down the chair and holds out his hands.*
JAMAL *cuts them free.*

MAHMOOD. Look, man, I'm freezing.

He shows his arm.

Goosebumps.

JAMAL. That's why it's called 'cold turkey'…

MAHMOOD. You've done this before.

JAMAL. You'll get the shakes and cramps and diarrhoea. It'll
stop around a week.

MAHMOOD. And then you'll let me go?

JAMAL. You want to do this, brother. You carry on like this,
you'll die.

MAHMOOD. I need a book.

JAMAL *takes a copy of the Qur'an from his pocket and
hands it to* MAHMOOD.

No, it's a special book.

JAMAL. This is a special book.

MAHMOOD. No. Another book. Tell Bernie and she'll get it
for us. It's from Waterstone's.

JAMAL. What, your slag kufr girlfriend buys books from
Waterstone's?

MAHMOOD. I need the book.

JAMAL. What for?

MAHMOOD. I need the book.

JAMAL. What for?

MAHMOOD. It's summat for my dad.

Scene Two

Citizenship tests. Actors come on to the stage, barking questions at the audience. Gradually, an instrumental version of 'Jerusalem' fades up behind them.

TERESA. Who is head of the Church of England?

FARZANA. How many members are there in the Welsh Assembly?

SYRUS. What is the distance from John O'Groats to Land's End?

TERESA. Choose either kilometres or miles.

ROBERT. What is the main function of the Council of Europe?

KIRSTY. Tip: Do not confuse the Council of Europe with the Council of the European Union.

SUSHIL. How can you find a dentist?

A moment.

IAN. Should a man be allowed to lock his wife or daughter in the house in order to prevent her disgracing him in public?

ROBERT. Where does the word 'Canada' come from?

IAN. What are the first three words of the US Constitution?

SUSHIL. When did the Danish women's national handball team win the world championships?

FARZANA. Name three low, German, mountain ranges.

A moment.

KIRSTY. What are the *two* key features of the civil service?

TERESA. What *two* rights are limited to US citizens?

SYRUS. What did Johannes Gutenberg invent?

IAN. What proportion of the UK population lives in Northern Ireland?

SUSHIL. Why does the flag have thirteen stripes?

ROBERT. List three ways in which you can protect the
environment.

FARZANA. Why did the Hugenots come to Britain in the
sixteenth and the eighteenth centuries?

KIRSTY. Which German composed the famous 'Ode to Joy' at
the end of his Ninth Symphony?

ROBERT. Which province has the most bilingual Canadians?

TERESA. Name one of the authors of the Federalist Papers?

SYRUS. How would you react if your adult son said that he
was homosexual?

IAN/FARZANA. Who do you go to if you have problems with
your neighbour?

*Enter an Asian woman in her thirties, dressed neatly in a
blue suit, with a clipboard. She is an* ASSISTANT
REGISTRAR.

Scene Three

*Citizenship ceremony. Council chamber. 'Jerusalem' continues.
A big photograph of the Queen, behind an arrangement of
flowers. A Union flag. Babies are crying, as they will throughout
the scene.*

ASSISTANT. Now, I realise that everyone is very excited about
what's about to happen.

An OFFICIAL *enters, and switches off the music.*

However, can everyone check – and if they've checked
already, *double*-check – that they've switched off all mobile
phones. Second, I need to point out the emergency exits,
which will be your means of exit in the event of an emergency. Now pray be upstanding for His Worship the Mayor.

Enter the MAYOR *in his regalia. He sits.*

Please be seated. Now, may I offer you a very warm welcome here, on behalf of the government, the Queen, Elizabeth the Second, and on behalf of the whole borough. Now, on your programme the introduction is by the Superintendant Registrar, so my first duty is to say that I regret that I am not the Superintendant Registrar but the Assistant Registrar, and it's my job to take you through the ceremony. But first I'd like to ask the Mayor to say a special word.

MAYOR. Ladies and gentlemen, boys and girls, it's my privilege to most sincerely welcome you to our magnificent, historic –

As the MAYOR *continues, we hear the imminent* CITIZENS *speaking charmingly, helpfully and largely incomprehensibly. This establishes the play's vernacular: ferocious doubling, casting across ethnic, age and sometimes gender, and only the most necessary elements of costume.*

HALIMA (*Somali*). *Wayan imi dalkan mayna yeelay wayood leehidin dowlad. Way wanaagsan tahay weliba in aad leedihiin free of speech and assembly and religion, oh yes please. Laakini ulma wagaagsana sida dowlanimadda. I am from Somalia.* [I didn't come to this country for community and diversity. I am all in favour of free of speech and assembly and religion, oh yes please. But they are not so good as government. I am from Somalia.]

CHONG (*Korean*). *Ah-tchik-too mah-nen han-gook kyo-poh-tul-nn New Malden-eh tsan-ni-tah. Ee-tchon-ee-nyon World Cup ter-nn semis eh-tson oo-ri-ka took-il tan-teh cho-sim-ni-tahj one nil-lo-yo. Yong-koo-too men-nal koo-ro-tcho. Citizenship test ta techuk-gu-eh kwan-hun kou-ra-myon nah-tchi-kum-tjim Duke of Edinburgh in-deh.* [For many of us, home is still New Malden. In the 2002 World Cup, we lose to Germany in the semis one-nil, but you're used to that. If the citizenship test is all on football I am now the Duke of Edinburgh.]

JASMINKA (*Albanian, Kosovo dialect*). *Edhe pse pagesa nuk eshte e mirē, unē erdha nē Bromley te'punoj dhe Keidesem pēr femijet e zoteriut Henderson, por ai po më vardiset. Pra unē e nderpreva punen. E tash une po evijoj coursin e gjuhes Angleze, cdo te'marte te-cilene udhehegin femrat te'cilat me*

*mesojnë mua personal empowerment dhe gjithashtu te-tregoj
se kush jam five foot five inches, 30-C bust, and I do not do
kissing, Greek or anything without a condom. Pra unë
mendoj, nese mundem mei theme këtogjiera pse unë nuk
mesoj me shumë ge ta marr posaporten e Britanis së Madhi
and sod this for a game of soldiers.* [I come in as au pair in
Bromley but the pay is bad and Mr Henderson doesn't keep
his hands to himself. So I end up working. But I go to an
English class on Tuesday run by group of ladies who teach
me personal empowerment and how to say that I am five foot
five inches, 30-C bust, and I do not do kissing, Greek or anything without a condom. And I think, if I can say all these
things, why don't I learn a bit more and get a British passport, and sod this for a game of soldiers.]

We hear the last words of the MAYOR's *speech:*

MAYOR. – once the ceremony is over, you will be as much a
citizen of the United Kingdom as anybody who was born
here. So, welcome to your new life here in our community.

ASSISTANT. Many thanks, Mr Mayor. Now we move on to the
ceremony proper. The first part is the oath, which is a promise
to be loyal and faithful to the Queen and her heirs. Now, those
of you who are going to swear the oath – those with blue
cards, please – and those with red cards, please stay seated.

Now, I need for you to state your names, one by one. Why
don't we start there with the lady.

The new CITIZENS *in a parade.* JAMAL, *a guest, standing
at the side.*

ISMENE (*Greek*). Ismene Christodoulakis.

JAMAL (*Arabic*). *Bism-illa al-rahman al-raheem.* [In the name
of Allah, the compassionate, the merciful.]

CHONG (*Korean*). Chong Myung Yoon.

JAMAL (*Arabic, quoting Sura 9:72-3 of the Qur'an*). *Wa'da
Allah al-móemeneen wal momenat janaat tagry men tahteha
al-anhaar –* ['God has promised the men and women who
believe in Him gardens watered by running streams –]

PERCY (*Zimbabwean*). Percy Tshabala.

JAMAL. – *khaldeen feeha*. [– in which they shall abide for ever.]

JASMINKA (*Kosovan*). Jasminka Hasani.

JAMAL. *Wa masaken tayebah fe janaat adn*. [Goodly mansions in the gardens of Eden…]

HALIMA (*Somali*). Halima Jama.

JAMAL. *Wa redwan men allah akbar*. [And, what is more, they shall have grace in God's sight.]

SAMIR. Samir Ibrahim.

JAMAL. *Zaleka howa al-fawz al-azeem*. [That is their supreme triumph.]

FATIMA (*Iranian, veiled*). Fatima Ahmed.

JAMAL. Prophet, make war on the unbelievers and the hypocrites –

TETYANA. Tetyana Ismael.

JAMAL. – and deal rigorously with them.

MAHMOOD (*Pakistani*). Mahmood Hussein.

JAMAL (*to* MAHMOOD). Hell shall be their home.

ASSISTANT. Thank you. Now please repeat the words after me. I swear by Almighty God –

RESPONSE. I swear by Almighty God –

ASSISTANT. – that, on becoming a British citizen –

RESPONSE. – that, on becoming a British citizen –

ASSISTANT. – I will be faithful and bear true allegiance –

RESPONSE. – I will be faithful and bear true allegiance –

ASSISTANT. – to Her Majesty Queen Elizabeth the Second –

RESPONSE. – to Her Majesty Queen Elizabeth the Second –

ASSISTANT. – Her Heirs and Successors according to law.

RESPONSE. – Her Heirs and Successors according to law.

ASSISTANT. I will give my loyalty –

The door crashes open. A middle-aged Pakistani man, AZIZ, bursts into the room.

AZIZ. Stop this.

MAYOR. Uh, what?

AZIZ. I know what's happening.

ASSISTANT. Please, what –

People running. Babies screaming.

MAYOR. You can't –

AZIZ. Where are you?

ASSISTANT. What do you want?

He tears off FATIMA*'s veil.*

MAYOR. No, you can't –

AZIZ. I know what you are doing here.

MAHMOOD. Hey, pal –

AZIZ. I know what you are doing now. Where are you?

Scene Four

ESOL (English for Speakers of Other Languages) class. EMMA *addressing a class.*

EMMA. So, stress. So, what is stress? One meaning:

She waves frantically, either side of her head.

Pressure. The other meaning: music. *La* la la la. People from Faiza to the window: One two three four. People from Zoran to the door: one and two and three and four.

Scene Five

Documentary. Citizenship blog.

BLOGGER. The new test for those wishing to become British citizens has been introduced. You buy a £9.99 book and take a £34 test, which seems a little steep for something with just twenty-four questions.

Scene Six

ESOL class. EMMA *addressing a class.*

EMMA (*claps on the stress*). *One – two – three – four.*

One and – *two* and – *three* and – four.

Now, door side: one two three four. Window side: one and a, two and a, three and a four.

She claps on the stress.

One – two – three – four.

One and a – *two* and a – *three* and a – four.

Scene Seven

Documentary. Citizenship blog.

BLOGGER. However, you can take it as many times as necessary, so centres will be falling over themselves to accept your cash.

Scene Eight

ESOL class.

EMMA. Now, window side, again: one two three four. Now at the same time, door side: one and then a, two and then a, three and then a four.

She claps on the stress.

One – two – three – four.

One and then a – *two* and then a – *three* and then a – *four*.

Scene Nine

Documentary. Citizenship blog.

BLOGGER. Somehow I have managed to be a British citizen for decades without knowing how long you have to be married before you can get divorced.

Scene Ten

ESOL class.

EMMA. So even though the window side is saying four things, and the door side is saying twelve things, it takes the same time because of the...

Stress wave.

...stress.

Scene Eleven

Workplace canteen. CHONG *and* DEREK. CHONG *reading.*
DEREK *leaning across.*

DEREK. Chong. Give it here.

Enter JOSHUA.

Chong. Give it here.

JOSHUA. Chong. Yoon.

DEREK. Chong. Give it here.

JOSHUA. Wassup?

DEREK. Chong Myung Yoon.

JOSHUA. Give it up.

Enter CHLOE.

DEREK. Chong, give it here.

JOSHUA. Give it to Derek.

CHLOE. Wassup?

DEREK. Chloe.

JOSHUA. Chong, give it to Derek.

DEREK. Chloe.

CHLOE. Give it to me.

CHONG *looks up to* CHLOE *and* JOSHUA *snatches the
book.* JOSHUA *looks it at, and throws it to* DEREK.

Wassup?

Scene Twelve

Home Office. Consultation. 1ST HISTORIAN *and* 2ND HISTORIAN.

1ST HISTORIAN. Let me make something clear. What the government is planning represents a golden opportunity, to call a halt to the long and baleful period of national apology. Can we stop pretending that there is no national narrative, and accept that Blenheim, Waterloo, El Alamein and, yes, the sacrifices of the Somme, all have their place in it. Can we acknowledge that while flags and trumpets are not everything, to define our greatest ages as Elizabethan or Victorian is not unconnected to the virtues of those monarchs. And can we, please, stop apologising for the British Empire.

2ND HISTORIAN. Let me say something at the outset. You will see people who will tell you that it's time to reassert a national narrative, stretching back into the mists of primitive antiquity. In fact, the British state as such – the union of England, Wales and Scotland, doesn't come about till 1707. The Irish are incorporated in 1800 and the United Kingdom as we have it dates from as late as 1921. The first named British institution is a bank. Our much-vaunted 'national story' is in fact a history of challenges to a hierarchic social order, from the peasants to the miners, from the English Revolution via the Chartists to the General Strike. Oh, and on ancient venerable traditions, the first dead British monarch to lie in state at Westminster isn't until 1910.

Scene Thirteen

Documentary. Citizenship blog.

'NICOLE'. and I just cant understand why the government need us to know the answer to such questions such as what percentage of the uk is under nineteen years of age, who is a shadow cabinet, and who can pass laws that british courts must enforce? I think the test is stupid.

Scene Fourteen

ESOL class. EMMA *is writing on a computerised whiteboard. What she writes appears on a computer. She writes: '1) Speaking, 2) The Past, 3) Electoral System, 4) Talking to the Visitors.' Her students today are* BABA *(Congolese),* HALIMA *(Somali),* DRAGOSLAV *(Serbian),* RANJIT *(Indian),* JASMINKA *(Kosovan) and* NASIM *(Egyptian).*

EMMA. Good morning. Did everybody have a good weekend?

But it rained. How might we say the same thing with the word 'although'?

That's right. But rain*ed*, and ha*d*. *Although* it rained, we *had* a good weekend. What did we talk about on Friday?

Winston Churchill. When did he die?

In relation to today.

Not today. Before.

Thumb over shoulder.

In the past. So our action words, like die, most likely end in 'd'. Like 'die*d*'.

Enter SAMIR *(Iranian).*

And here's Samir, who had a *particularly* good weekend.

SAMIR. Forgive me please.

EMMA. Samir *is* late. And he *was* late on Friday.

SAMIR. So sorry.

EMMA. And he *will* be on time on Wednesday. 'Will' is what kind of word?

BABA. Bossy.

EMMA. Could be. But…

EMMA *points.*

RANJIT. Future.

EMMA. A future word. We will all be on time for our ESOL class on Wednesday.

EMMA 2. ESOL means 'English for Speakers of Other Languages'. It used to be 'English as a Second Language', ESL, which implied that people were monolingual before. Like the English.

EMMA. And if Samir was late last week and is late today, how should we start the sentence 'next time' will be different?

SAMIR. I have appointment.

EMMA. Ha*d*.

RANJIT. 'Although.'

SAMIR. I had appointment.

EMMA. I know. And although it is not good to be late, it is good that you are here. Now, back to Winston Churchill. And what he di*d* – before.

EMMA 2. There are two ways to meet the citizenship and language requirements to be naturalised. One is to pass a test taken on a computer at a testing centre, which requires you to have read and studied a book called *Life in the UK*. Which we think is pretty hard, even though they've produced a revised and simpler version of the book. Have you read the revised and simpler version of the book?

Scene Fifteen

Documentary. The 1ST *and* 2ND EDITION*S of the* Life in the UK *handbook.*

1ST EDITION. 'To understand a country well and the character of its inhabitants, some history is needed. We are influenced more than we imagine by images of the past, true or false, historical or legendary.'

2ND EDITION. 'To understand a country it is important to know something about its history.'

1ST EDITION. 'In 1707 came the Act of Union with Scotland.'

2ND EDITION. 'The English put pressure on the Scots to join England in an Act of Union.'

1ST EDITION. 'To some degree the English tolerance of different national cultures in the United Kingdom itself may have influenced the character of their imperial rule in India.'

2ND EDITION. Mm.

Scene Sixteen

ESOL class.

EMMA 2. The other route is to complete an ESOL course with a citizenship component. So you don't have to take the test.

EMMA. He *was* prime minister, not president. Not just of England. But of what?

DRAGOSLAV. UK.

BABA. United Kingdom.

EMMA. The UK doesn't have a president. Later we *will* discuss if it *might* – maybe word – be best to have a president, instead of what we have which is…

EMMA 2. Which is what my group is doing here today.

HALIMA. The Queen.

EMMA. The Queen, indeed. But first, today is special. We have visitors.

Applause.

They are from the theatre. What does 'theatre' mean?

HALIMA. Big place.

EMMA. That's right.

JASMINKA. For dance and sing.

EMMA. Singing and dancing.

RANJIT. Laughter.

EMMA. Yes. A big place, where people go for fun and entertainment.

EMMA 2. So, no pressure there.

EMMA *does her 'stress' gesture.*

Scene Seventeen

Child's bedroom. TETYANA *is at a computer.* MUNA *(11) is asleep in the corner.* TETYANA 2 *is what* TETYANA *is typing.* AZIZ *calls from offstage.*

TETYANA 2. Ismael. Tetyana Mikhailovna.

AZIZ (*offstage*). Tina!

TETYANA 2. 160a, Balsall Heath Park Road, Birmingham.

AZIZ (*offstage*). Tina, where are you now?

TETYANA 2. Female.

AZIZ (*offstage*). Where are you?

TETYANA 2. Married.

AZIZ (*offstage*). Tina!

TETYANA (*calls*). Aziz, I look after Muna!

MUNA *turns over in her sleep.*

(*Reads.*) 'If your application is approved, you will need to take part in a ceremony. If you want it in another area…' You bet.

TETYANA 2. London.

AZIZ (*offstage*). What you doing?

TETYANA (*calls*). Car insurance!

TETYANA 2 (*out of the air*). King's Cross Station.

AZIZ (*offstage*). I go out now!

TETYANA 2. Ismael, Aziz. Twenty-three – six – nineteen-seventy. Mirpur.

TETYANA (*calls*). I look after Muna!…

(*Reads.*) 'Dates places of your husband's wife's civil partner's previous marriage civil partnership. Dates places and reasons for ending of your husband's wife's civil partner's previous marriage or civil partnership, if applicable.'

Bit problem here you see. It all depend.

(*To the computer.*) Back home in Pakistan, they think he still marry to his first wife, who runs off with driving teacher, no surprise, now is fuck knows where. In Oldham his many cousins think I am good loyal devout Mirpuri girl but so sad, agrophobia, but maybe Christmas holidays we come make visit. In Newcastle-in-Lyne more other cousins know I am me, Ukraine Orthodox, oh so terrible, but is good because he make announce I plan to make revert not convert, because apparently, big story, everybody Muslim under skin. But big problem, if I am not British citizen, any time he can say we are sham marriage and hey-ho British government send me back to Dnepropetrovsk.

Door slam off.

(*Calls.*) Aziz!

MUNA *turns over.*

Actually it in fact sham marriage, more or less.

(*Quieter call.*) Aziz!

Changes computer programme.

Yo.

(*Reads.*) 'Hear this screen.'

Scene Eighteen

Workplace canteen. DEREK *has* CHONG's *book.* CHLOE *and* JOSHUA *are watching.*

DEREK. Newspapers are not allowed to express political opinions. True or false?

CHONG. Give me the book.

DEREK. True or false?

CHONG. True.

CHLOE. And our survey said…

DEREK *does a klaxon noise and tosses the book to* CHLOE.

JOSHUA. I know that.

DEREK. Chlo.

CHLOE. So, 'Why did Jews come to Britain in the early years of the twentieth century? Was it (A) to escape famine, (B) to escape persecution, (C) to make a better life, or (D) to avoid military service?'

JOSHUA. Or (E) support a rubbish football team.

DEREK. Naughty. Chong?

CHONG. To make better life.

DEREK. Which was?

CHONG. C. Give it here.

JOSHUA. And is that right?

DEREK. No, actually, they came here to escape from persecution.

CHLOE. So what's the pass rate?

DEREK. What's the pass rate, Chong?

CHONG. I don't know. Give it here.

Scene Nineteen

Child's bedroom. The WEBSITE *is speaking to* TETYANA.
MUNA *sleeps.*

WEBSITE. This navigation tutorial helps you to find your way
    around the Life in the UK Test...

> MUNA *turns over, makes a slight noise.*

...and gives you the chance to practise answering some
    simple questions. These questions are just for fun, but will
    help you understand how to answer questions on a computer.

Scene Twenty

ESOL class. EMMA *and* TOBY, *a volunteer. On the board, the
words 'Society, Community, Respect, Government, Values,
Morality, Charity, Freedom, Diversity, Justice'. Students are*
HALIMA, JASMINKA, BABA, RANJIT, DRAGOSLAV *and*
NASIM. TOBY *is handing round a sheet.*

EMMA. What can be happening? What is Toby doing?

BABA. Toby hand out paper.

EMMA. Toby is handing out sheets of paper. 'Ing' words?

HALIMA. 'Now' words.

EMMA. Now, but lo-o-o-ng. He is hand*ing* the list to Jasminka,
    to Baba, to Dragoslav. The pictures are things you can *do* to
    be a good citizen. There is a list of words which describe the
    doing things.

TOBY. On the back.

EMMA. When you go home, you match the list to the pictures
    and bring it back on Friday.

BABA. Emma, this picture.

EMMA. It's a ballot box. Does anyone know what a ballot box is?

JASMINKA. For vote.

EMMA. For vot*ing*.

BABA. Lo-o-o-ong.

HALIMA. For ever.

TOBY. So they say.

RANJIT. And this?

EMMA (*after a glance*). Good question. But the pictures you
will do at home.

She points.

JASMINKA. Tomorrow word.

EMMA. Prediction. What will happen. But also 'You will do it'
means…

DRAGOSLAV. Must do.

EMMA. Exactly. Bossy word. 'You must.' 'It's an order.' Now,
today we discuss these words. Vocabulary. Discuss?

NASIM is looking at the pictures she's been handed.

HALIMA. Talking.

BABA. To-and-fro.

EMMA. And what phrases help for discussing to-and-fro?

BABA. Be polite.

EMMA. Phrases to show you are polite. Halima.

HALIMA. Please and thank you.

JASMINKA. Beg your pardon.

EMMA. Good. In discussion?

BABA. Please excuse me.

EMMA. Good.

HALIMA. Forgive me please.

EMMA. Excellent.

DRAGOSLAV. Matter of fact.

EMMA. Maybe… 'As a matter of fact.' Or, 'In my opinion.' Or, 'In my view.'

RANJIT. Live and let live.

EMMA. If you like.

JASMINKA. Mind your own business.

EMMA. Well…

RANJIT. Play up and play the game.

BABA. And keep your to…

TOBY. Keep yourself to…

BABA. To yourself.

EMMA. And of course I see your…

JASMINKA. Point.

HALIMA. Good point.

EMMA. Or another sort of point?

BABA. Fair point.

EMMA. Or fair…

RANJIT. Fair view?

EMMA. Fair enough. But even so…

DRAGOSLAV. But in my fair view with most respect I must say what you talk is quite baloney.

EMMA. Brilliant. 'In my view.' 'View' means?

RANJIT. Opinion.

EMMA. But it can also mean…

Shading eyes.

HALIMA. Look.

EMMA. And…

Gestures across the group.

BABA. ESOL class.

EMMA. When you look, what you see. My view.

DRAGOSLAV. See where you come from.

EMMA. Excellent.

BABA. If you ask me.

EMMA (*wiggles her ear*). And what d'you do with this?

HALIMA. Listen.

DRAGOSLAV. Listen up.

EMMA. Yes, or put another way, you *hear*.

DRAGOSLAV. 'I hear you.'

EMMA. Yes, which means – Although I have heard – hear*d* –
your view, your opinion, this is mine.

DRAGOSLAV. All great baloney.

JASMINKA. What is baloney?

EMMA. Let us concentrate on using all those phrases when
we discuss which things are most important to becoming a
good citizen.

HALIMA. To be citizen you must pass course and say oath to
the Queen.

EMMA. 'Must.' Bossy. Good.

DRAGOSLAV. Like Queen.

EMMA. And to pass the course you must discuss these words.
Nasim.

NASIM. Yes?

EMMA. Maybe you could start us off.

NASIM. Start you off?

EMMA. To discuss the importance of these words.

Scene Twenty-One

Documentary. Citizenship blog.

TRAON SOFTWARE. I am here to show you a revolutionary new program directed at thoise attemping to becom British citizens, in short it is an expertly researched revision tool, compiled using chapters 2,3,4 of the 'A road to British Citizenship' (2nd edition). This program is available from my web site: www.traon.co.uk

Scene Twenty-Two

Top-floor room. JAMAL stands. MAHMOOD's girlfriend BERNIE stands with a plastic bag on her head, carrying another plastic bag and her handbag. MAHMOOD is rolling gently on the floor.

BERNIE. So can I take this off?

MAHMOOD. Oh shit.

BERNIE. Can I take this off?

MAHMOOD. Bernie, I've got the fucking shits.

BERNIE. This is like a Tarantino.

JAMAL. You can take it off.

MAHMOOD. Bernie, my stomach's, like, exploding.

    BERNIE *takes her bag off, and sees* MAHMOOD.

BERNIE. Oh, Maz. Cupcake. You look terrible.

MAHMOOD. Mahmood.

BERNIE. You what?

MAHMOOD. I feel terrible.

JAMAL. Mahmood. His name.

BERNIE. Ay, 'tis. You going?

MAHMOOD. I got the cramps.

JAMAL. 'Course I aren't going.

BERNIE. You aren't going?

MAHMOOD. Chuffing ada.

JAMAL. One plonker comes round, like 'me best friend' of some other bloke, and he leaves wraps and that stuffed up all the taps. What's the point of that?

BERNIE. OK, then search me.

JAMAL. No way.

BERNIE. You wanna know I'm clean, you search me.

JAMAL. No way.

    BERNIE *starts to take her clothes off, hurling them at* JAMAL.

BERNIE. OK then, search my clothes.

JAMAL. Stop that.

BERNIE. You don't have to touch me.

MAHMOOD. Bernie.

BERNIE. You've just to touch my clothes.

MAHMOOD. Chuffing hell, Bernie…

JAMAL. OK.

    BERNIE *stops undressing*.

    OK. Your bag.

    BERNIE *goes and gives him her bag*, JAMAL *looking away*.

    What's in the other bag?

    She picks up the bag and upends it. Food and two books fall out.

BERNIE. Hummus. Raspberry and banana smoothie. Ice cream. Gone bit runny.

JAMAL. Books.

BERNIE. Oh, yes. 'Flying out of third-floor windows for beginners.' 'Five easy places to conceal smack in bedsits.' 'How to manufacture crack from mats.'

JAMAL goes and picks up the food.

JAMAL. You've ten minutes. Tell her what you want of her.

JAMAL goes out.

BERNIE. Cupcake.

MAHMOOD. Bernie, I feel real bad.

BERNIE. So, whatcha 'want of me'?

MAHMOOD. Dunno as I can do this…

BERNIE. What's he mean, 'you want of me'?

MAHMOOD. He wants me to have you revert, like.

BERNIE. Revert? What to?

MAHMOOD. Like, to Islam.

BERNIE. I'm not a Muslim – how the fuck do I revert to Islam?

MAHMOOD. I can't explain.

BERNIE. No, I bet you can't.

MAHMOOD. I've just –

BERNIE. My cousin Isabel's off with an Asian lad. He had her cut up her CDs.

MAHMOOD. Ay, well…

BERNIE. And now she's calling herself Nimaat and saying dancing's sex with clothes on.

MAHMOOD. Ah, well. Anyway…

BERNIE. And you think I'm right for / turning Muslim –

MAHMOOD. Bernie, I can't do a week / of this…

BERNIE. Cupcake, I don't give a shit if you're Maz or Mahmood or Mohammad s'long as you're off this.

Pause.

MAHMOOD. So you're gonna leave me here?

Slight pause.

BERNIE. So what's these then?

MAHMOOD. You're gonna leave me here?

BERNIE. These books you wanted.

MAHMOOD. S'for me dad, like.

BERNIE. What's for your dad?

MAHMOOD. I need your help.

BERNIE. No, Micky, I / can't get you...

MAHMOOD. My dad thinks I'm a British citizen.

BERNIE. What, your dad in Pakistan?

MAHMOOD. I don't have no other dad.

BERNIE. You in't a British citizen?

MAHMOOD. He never gets me citizenship, before I were
    eighteen. My brothers got it when you didn't have to take
    the test.

BERNIE. The test.

MAHMOOD. Now he's gone back home It Is His Dearest Wish.

BERNIE. The test.

MAHMOOD. I said I passed it.

BERNIE. What test, like?

MAHMOOD. Now he wants a picture from the ceremony.

BERNIE. What ceremony?

MAHMOOD. So I've got to pass it.

Slight pause.

BERNIE. Oh?

MAHMOOD. He thinks I'm at Leeds Met and all. Reading English Literature. He asks us all about John Milton and Jane Austen.

BERNIE. Oh, ay?

MAHMOOD. I failed the test. I didn't read this book. We have to read this book and then you ask me questions from the other one. We can do it while I'm here.

He opens a book and reads:

'What is the national day for England?'

He holds the book out to her.

S'easy. All you have to do is read the questions.

A moment. He looks at the book, puts his thumb on the place, holds it out to her. She looks at the page and shakes her head.

BERNIE. Cupcake. T'int that easy.

MAHMOOD. Just read the questions.

BERNIE. Cupcake, there's some things I can't do for you.

Scene Twenty-Three

Child's bedroom. MAHMOOD *still there. The* WEBSITE *is testing* TETYANA.

WEBSITE. The first type of question involves selecting one correct answer from four options.

TETYANA/WEBSITE. Where is the prime minister's official home in London?

WEBSITE. Downing Street, Parliament Square, Richmond Terrace, Whitehall Place.

TETYANA. I suppose to know this?

WEBSITE. The next type of question involves deciding whether a statement is true or false. Citizens of the UK can vote in elections at the age of eighteen. True or false.

TETYANA. True.

WEBSITE. The next question type involves selecting *two* correct answers from four options. You should not select more or fewer answers than this!

Scene Twenty-Four

ESOL class. EMMA, TOBY, HALIMA, JASMINKA, BABA, RANJIT, DRAGOSLAV *and* NASIM.

RANJIT. If you ask me, community is most important as a common bond of people share one place.

EMMA. And 'society'? What is the difference between community and society?

Pause.

'Between.' This or that. The difference of that from this.

JASMINKA. In my view maybe society… is many small, add up to big.

EMMA. You mean that all our communities / add up –

TOBY. Our diverse communities.

EMMA. Good, good. And what about diversity?

Pause.

Well, in my opinion…

She waves round the class.

BABA. ESOL class.

EMMA. Exactly. Indian, and Serbia, the Congo…

Gesture to JASINKA.

JASINKA. Kosova.

EMMA. Of course. And / Egypt…

DRAGOSLAV (*muttered in Serbian*). *Nema zemlje Kosovo.*
[There is no country called Kosovo.]

EMMA. In English please, and I've missed somebody...

DRAGOSLAV. I say that Kosovo is not a country.

EMMA. Good example. Many differing opinions.

DRAGOSLAV. Forgive me say this, please.

EMMA. Which is what happens when you have diverse communities.

HALIMA. I am so very sorry but is my opinion... I come to this country not for community diversity.

EMMA. Came. Go on.

HALIMA. Good free of speech and assembly and religion, oh yes please. But most big matter, most...

TOBY. Important thing.

HALIMA. Yes, important thing is government. I am from Somalia.

EMMA. Well, point taken. And 'values'. What are values?

RANJIT. I thinking if you ask me...

EMMA. Yes?

RANJIT. Values is all the words.

EMMA. 'Respect.' 'Freedom.' 'Justice.' Yes. Great point.

  Pause.

  Are there any values that aren't there?

  Slight pause.

BABA. Religion.

JASMINKA. Parliament Westminster.

EMMA. Well, democracy's a value.

TOBY. Equality.

EMMA. Good. What is equality?

RANJIT. Everybody is the same.

EMMA. Treated the same. So, for example, in this college, men and women are all paid the same for doing the same job. Paid equally.

Pause. The learners look at each other.

Except for Toby, who's a volunteer, so he doesn't get paid anything. Aaah.

ALL (*echoing*). Aaah.

HALIMA. Beg pardon. You mean you pay same as Mr Chlebowski?

EMMA. Is this so terrible?

HALIMA. But you have husband.

EMMA. Do you think that makes a difference?

Pause.

RANJIT. In UK, the most rich person is the Queen.

EMMA. Some people think we shouldn't have a queen. That the monarchy – having kings and queens – is rather old-fashioned and outdated. Perhaps some of you agree with that?

The learners look at each other.

Well, fair enough. As Halima reminded us, you'll all be swearing oaths to be loyal to the Queen. So, moving quickly on to 'Justice' and 'Respect'…

TOBY *nudges her.* NASIM *is holding up her handout.*

Ah, Nasim.

NASIM. You say we must take these pictures home.

EMMA. Yes, to choose the right words from the list.

NASIM. I cannot take these pictures home into my house. Forgive me please.

She stands, takes the pictures to EMMA, *and hands them to her.*

EMMA. Well, if…

NASIM (*turning to* DRAGOSLAV). You are Serbia?

DRAGOSLAV *nods*.

So many of my people die in Bosnia and Kosova.

Scene Twenty-Five

Home Office. Consultation: 3RD HISTORIAN.

3RD HISTORIAN. Now, look. I know what they've been
    telling you. The ancient and venerable tradition, versus a
    bitter history of struggle and revolt. And of course it's more
    than drums and muskets and the Virgin Queen. But nor is it
    just revolting peasants, lurking in their hovel and considering
    which machines to wreck. Neither maps and chaps nor looms
    and gloom. But an unrolling and unfurling of our democratic
    liberties. A golden thread, which runs from Magna Carta via
    the Reformation and the Bill of Rights, to the ending of the
    slave trade, Catholic emancipation, the reform acts and uni-
    versal suffrage. The democratic citizen, throwing off the
    chains of superstition, tyranny and prejudice.

Scene Twenty-Six

Dinner party. EMMA, IAN, PAULINE *(thirties)*, MARTIN
(fifties).

EMMA. I just resent the idea you can read everything about
    anybody off their postcode.

PAULINE. All I'm saying is…

EMMA. I live in Slough so naturally I eat out and buy small
    appliances. I run a reconditioned BMW so I must be black.

PAULINE. All I'm saying is…

EMMA. I rent DVDs and I'm resident in Rhyl so of course
    I'm vegetarian.

IAN. But you are vegetarian.

EMMA. I'm not vegetarian.

IAN (*re: the food*). Am I missing something?

EMMA. My sister's vegetarian.

PAULINE. Yes, actually, / he knows –

EMMA. Odd that, because she watches *Lost* and runs an Audi.

PAULINE. Watching *Lost* is compatible with being vegetarian.

MARTIN. What did you call us?

EMMA. 'Urban Intelligentsia.'

PAULINE. All I'm saying is…

MARTIN. And that's a 'tribe' consisting of, what? Just over five per cent of the British population?

PAULINE. Seven. All I'm saying is…

EMMA. So I pop into Iceland for some Diet Coke. So suddenly I eat Twizzlers, shop at TK Maxx and holiday in Minehead in a caravan?

MARTIN. I have owned a caravan.

EMMA (*re:* PAULINE). We have / owned a –

MARTIN. Well, a camper van.

EMMA (*re:* PAULINE). We have owned a camper van.

IAN. But…

PAULINE. We owned a camper van when we were growing up.

IAN. Doesn't that imply that camper vans / aren't quite the same…

EMMA. So what does that make / us?

PAULINE. When we, or rather you and Dad, thought the world divided into two.

MARTIN. You see…

PAULINE. The heroic this, the oppressive that.

EMMA. You see…

PAULINE. All I'm saying is, that if you live in Hornchurch and believe in common sense and occupy a crescent property with carriage lamps and possess an M&S card, then it's unlikely that you'll read the *Guardian*.

EMMA. I see. And there's some kind of law that everybody who opposes global warming or eats hummus or wears Birkenstocks has to holiday in Tuscany?

PAULINE. Well, the crespelli were to die for. Where did you get the fresh beetroot for the borscht? And what *is* this fruity little number with its cigar-box notes and undertones of raspberry?

EMMA. It's just a Cabernet. / Martin brought it.

MARTIN. I bought it.

PAULINE. From?

EMMA (*looks*). Lebanon.

PAULINE. As it is nearly time for *Newsnight*. Welcome to the tribe.

MARTIN. But I'm not a tribe. It's Monday, I'm a teacher. Saturday, I'm a Spurs supporter. Thursday, I'm a Labour voter. Friday, I'm a man.

PAULINE. But that's what your tribe does. It sits in Starbucks, with its latte and its laptop, wondering where to go today.

IAN. Of course, you might say / that the very –

MARTIN. Not a latte.

EMMA. And not fucking Starbucks.

PAULINE. Well, I rest my case.

IAN. I suppose the issue is, whether what you purchase actually / determines all the other –

PAULINE (*writing on a napkin, speaking to* MARTIN). What's the most important, non-personal, public-event-type formative happening in your young life? You're not allowed the World Cup.

Hands the napkin to IAN.

MARTIN. Well, I suppose it would have to be the events in / Paris –

PAULINE. You don't even have to go there.

IAN (*holding up the napkin*). Paris May Sixty-fucking-eight.

Pause.

PAULINE. You've probably convinced yourself that you were there. The greatest event in the entire history of everything.

Pause.

MARTIN. Of course, I realise it wouldn't look that way to you.

PAULINE. And what if, Wednesday, you're a Muslim?

Scene Twenty-Seven

Documentary: Citizenship blog/Child's bedroom/Top-floor room. The WEBSITE *is testing* TETYANA. MAHMOOD *sits on the floor.*

WEBSITE. Where have migrants come from in the past and why? What sort of work have they done?

MAHMOOD. Jamal! Jamal!

'HAMID'. This test won't bother me cause i have to read too many harder books for uni, but i cant imagin what my friends will do who can hardly spell BRITISH word.

Scene Twenty-Eight

Dinner party. Soliloquy: MARTIN.

MARTIN 2. I was nineteen when the events in Paris happened. In
fact, yes, I had driven over, in a Morris Minor Thousand, the
estate, with wood framing on the rear bodywork. In that kind
of situation, it takes a while to find out where it's at. I spent the
first night on the streets and the second in the Odeon, which
had been occupied, and where we were addressed by Goddard,
Sartre and maybe Jean Genet. Someone painted graffiti on the
Morris: '*La revolution est incroyable parce que vraie.*' I didn't
ever wash it off. Feeling in England the most lunatic of
fringes. Seeing how many of us there actually were.

Slight pause.

And you know what? If you asked me, what would this –
thing we wanted, this utopia, this 'socialism', what it would
actually feel like? Equality, emancipation, liberation? The
unlocking of the great infinity of human possibility? I'd say:
that day.

MARTIN *turns to* PAULINE.

Of course, I realise it wouldn't look that way to you.

Scene Twenty-Nine

*Documentary: Citizenship blog/Child's bedroom/Top-floor
room. The* WEBSITE *is testing* TETYANA. MAHMOOD *sits
on the floor.*

'NASIMA'. after geting A+ on my first semester in english A
levels i have fail the test. i do not thing this is such a great idea.

WEBSITE. How many children live in single-parent families?

MAHMOOD. Jamal! Come here!

WEBSITE. What is the minimum ages for buying alcohol and
tobacco?

'ROSE'. I have lived here since i was 7 years old and believe
that people who have lived here for such a long time should
not have to take any test. i hope I pass as I haven't got £34.00
to waste and plus i want to go on holiday for 10th July

Enter JAMAL *to* MAHMOOD. *Enter* MUNA *to stand
behind* TETYANA.

JAMAL. Yeah, what?

WEBSITE. What rights do the citizens of EU states have to
work and travel?

Scene Thirty

Top-floor room. JAMAL *and* MAHMOOD.

MAHMOOD. I want you to ask me summat.

JAMAL. Ask you what?

MAHMOOD *gives him the book.*

MAHMOOD. It's like a quiz.

JAMAL. What quiz?

He looks at the book:

'You need a separate television licence for every television,
DVD, video recorder or computer in your house.' This is all
shit, man.

MAHMOOD. Like, true or false.

JAMAL. (A) True. (B) False.

MAHMOOD. B. False. You've to check the answer. It's a
number at the back.

JAMAL. B. False. Right answer.

MAHMOOD. Next.

JAMAL. This is all shit, man.

MAHMOOD. Please. Next.

JAMAL. 'When can you drink alcohol in a pub or enter a betting shop or gambling club?' The answer's never, it's *haram*.

MAHMOOD. Not for British people, gimme the options.

JAMAL. Can't see why you're doing this.

MAHMOOD. Gimme the chuffing options.

JAMAL. (A) Twenty-one, (B) eighteen, (C) sixteen, (D) twelve.

MAHMOOD. Eighteen. B.

JAMAL looks at the answer.

JAMAL. Eighteen. B. Correct.

MAHMOOD. Next question.

JAMAL. 'Possessing cannabis, amphetamines, cocaine and heroin's illegal. True or false?'

MAHMOOD. Ask me another.

JAMAL. Why are you doing this?

MAHMOOD. I said. It's for my dad.

JAMAL. I thought your dad went back to Pakistan.

MAHMOOD. That's why.

JAMAL. That's *why*?

Slight pause.

MAHMOOD. He says if I'm a British citizen then when he dies my cousins out in Pakistan can't have me thrown in jail when I go back to claim the house. I guess for you that all sounds pretty fucking crazy.

Scene Thirty-One

Top-floor room. Soliloquy: MAHMOOD.

MAHMOOD 2. He allus said as how you couldn't understand the British till you'd borrowed cups of sugar over garden

fences or took holidays in Morecambe. He took me to the
place near Keighley where there's this little house where
three sisters all wrote books in tiny books, and the garden
leads into a cemetery. He told me the difference 'tween
church and chapel. How dukes are up from earls and earls are
up from marquises. And how the British ruled the waves and
minded their own business and was gonna fight the Germans
on the beaches and the landing grounds in their finest hour.

(*To* JAMAL.) I guess for you that all sounds pretty fucking
crazy.

Scene Thirty-Two

Workplace canteen. DEREK *has* CHONG*'s book.* CHLOE *and*
JOSHUA *are watching.*

CHONG. Three-quarters of the questions right.

DEREK. What is?

CHONG. The pass rate.

CHLOE. No chance.

DEREK. Looks like we're going to have to send you back to
Fook In A-dar. Josh. You're Bamber Gascoigne.

DEREK *tosses the book to* JOSHUA.

JOSHUA. 'Which of these statements is correct? (A) In the
nineteenth century, women had fewer rights than men. (B)
Women have always had the same rights as men.'

DEREK. Or, (C) Now women have a lot more rights than men.
Which is why / I wanna fucking emigrate.

CHONG. A.

CHLOE. Yes?

JOSHUA. We might have to keep you after all.

CHLOE *gestures for the book.* JOSHUA *tosses it to her.*
CHONG *tries to intercept.*

DEREK. Now now. Hard question.

CHLOE. Does it say?

DEREK. Just ask him a hard question.

CHLOE. 'Where is Gaelic spoken? Cornwall, Northumberland, or – '

DEREK. Cricklewood.

CHLOE. Or –

CHONG. Is Cornwall.

JOSHUA. Uh…

DEREK. Right. What is the capital of Scotland? Is it (A) Penzance or (B) Aberystwyth.

CHONG. Aberystwyth.

JOSHUA. Hey –

CHLOE. Correct. 'Which of these statements is correct? (A) Bonfire Night commemorates the Battle of Trafalgar. (B) Bonfire Night commemorates the winning of the First World War.'

JOSHUA. Uh…

CHONG. B.

CHLOE. Full marks. And the Grand National is a football game. A tennis tournament. A concert hall. Or a…

DEREK. Public holiday.

JOSHUA. Uh…?

DEREK. Or a cocktail or a motorway.

JOSHUA. It's not…

DEREK. Now, Joshua. No helping.

Scene Thirty-Three

Child's bedroom. TETYANA *at the computer.* MUNA *stands behind her, looking at the screen.*

TETYANA. It is a race for horses.

MUNA. What is?

TETYANA. Hey, Muna. You must be sleep.

MUNA. The computer's talking.

TETYANA. Yes, so sorry.

MUNA. What's all this?

TETYANA. It's quiz. For fun.

WEBSITE. Where are Geordie, Cockney and Scouse spoken?

TETYANA. Uh – beats me.

MUNA. Cockney is London.

TETYANA. There is different language in King's Cross?

WEBSITE. What languages other than English are spoken in Northern Ireland, Scotland and Wales?

TETYANA. I don't know that either.

MUNA. In Wales, people speak in Wales.

TETYANA. Obviously.

MUNA. No, in a language.

TETYANA. Do they?

MUNA. Where's my daddy?

TETYANA. Out. At Madjit's you bet. Maybe we play quiz together.

MUNA. Why are you doing this?

TETYANA. I say, for fun.

MUNA. Does Daddy know you're doing this?

TETYANA (*giving* MUNA *the book*). No. It must be secret.

MUNA. 'K…

WEBSITE. Where does the prime minister live?

TETYANA. Easy. I look this up in book, *Life in UK*. Is
    Downing Square.

Scene Thirty-Four

ESOL class. Tutorial. TOBY, JASMINKA *and* NASIM.

TOBY. I'm recording this, so we can listen afterwards and
    correct it. So, I would say: 'Hello, my name is… Toby, and
    this is my colleague… Hannah.' In this first part of the exam-
    ination, you are going to ask and answer some questions.
    What is your name?

JASMINKA. Jasminka Hasani.

TOBY. What is your name?

NASIM. Nasim Dad.

TOBY. Where do you come from?

JASMINKA. I from Kosova.

TOBY. I *am* from Kosova. Where do you come from?

NASIM. I *am* from Egypt.

TOBY. Good. Now, the next thing you'll be asked to do is ask
    each other questions on a topic that will be chosen for you.
    Nasim, can you ask Jasminka about the television pro-
    grammes she likes watching?

    Slight pause.

    If you like, you can take some time to write down the
    questions.

NASIM. What about the television programmes you like
    watching?

TOBY. I think you'd say: 'What television programmes do you like?'

JASMINKA. I like to watch *Casualty*, *X-Factor* and *I Am Celebrity Please Get Me Out Of Here*.

TOBY. Good.

Slight pause.

(*To* NASIM.) Now you ask another question.

NASIM. What about?

TOBY. About any of these programmes.

NASIM. I have never seen these programmes.

Pause.

TOBY. OK. Jasminka. I'd like you to ask Nasim her opinion about famous people. You can spend a moment writing down the questions.

JASMINKA *notes for a moment. Then:*

JASMINKA. Please tell me, in your opinion, what famous people do you admire?

NASIM. British people?

JASMINKA *looks at* TOBY.

TOBY. Not necessarily.

JASMINKA. Not necessarily.

NASIM. You mean film stars?

JASMINKA. I don't know.

TOBY. Or sportsmen. Politicians.

NASIM. You want I give my opinion about George Bush and Tony Blair?

TOBY. I want you to pass speaking and listening at ESOL Entry Three. That may not be the topic.

Checks notes for another topic.

Jasminka, why not ask Nasim about her future hopes and plans.

JASMINKA. Why not?

TOBY. I mean, ask Nasim about her future hopes and plans. If you want to, you can write down / the questions –

JASMINKA. What are your future hopes and plans?

NASIM. For me as person?

JASMINKA. Yes.

TOBY. For you and your family.

JASMINKA. And for you and your family.

TOBY. Jobs, or holidays…

NASIM. You mean the family of my religion?

TOBY. I think Jasminka shares / your religion –

NASIM. I wish for right to live by laws of my religion.

TOBY. Yup.

Pause.

OK, now, Jasminka. You ask her what she means.

Scene Thirty-Five

Dinner party/ESOL class.

MARTIN. They don't mean cutting people's hands off.

PAULINE. Oh, no?

MARTIN. They mean interest-free mortgages.

PAULINE. Oh, right.

EMMA. They have a system.

PAULINE. / So…

EMMA. So they can borrow without it technically being / usury.

PAULINE. So when whatever staggering percentage / of young Muslim men –

MARTIN. It's not just / mortgages.

PAULINE. – whatever staggering percentage / says they want to live under Sharia law, it's really just as an alternative to the Abbey National?

NASIM *appears*.

NASIM. Mrs Goodman-Lee?

EMMA. In fact, it's only like, it's equivalent to asking / a committed Christian –

NASIM. Mrs Goodman-Lee?

EMMA. – if they'd like to live under God's law.

PAULINE. 'Equivalent'?

NASIM. Mrs –

EMMA. Nasim, I'll be with you in a moment.

PAULINE. Did you say 'equivalent'?

EMMA. I said, equivalent to asking / a committed –

PAULINE. 'Cos shoot me down in flames on this, but my understanding is, that under this particular / God's law –

EMMA. If you asked someone who was / a committed Christian if –

PAULINE. – gay sex is an abomination.

IAN. In fact, most of the other major world / religions –

PAULINE. And that if you're a Muslim man you have a right, a duty / to beat up your –

MARTIN. Have you read Leviticus?

PAULINE. No, not / recently.

MARTIN. Leviticus is pretty unambigious on sodomy.

PAULINE. So is the C of E seeking to impose ecclesiastical law on Ponders End?

MARTIN. I don't think they're wanting to impose anything on all of anywhere.

PAULINE. On parts of Ponders End?

MARTIN. I mean, it's not for everybody. Just for Muslims.

PAULINE. Oh, fine. So you can throw gay Muslims off the sides of mountains in some parts / of Ponders End.

IAN. And it's actually voluntary.

PAULINE. But only if you really want to.

NASIM. Mrs Goodman-Lee, I want to speak to you.

IAN. And isn't there the Jewish thing?

PAULINE. What / Jewish thing?

EMMA. In a moment.

MARTIN. Yes, you know, the Jewish thing.

PAULINE. What Jewish thing?

NASIM. Shall I go up to your office?

IAN. How far you can walk on the Sabbath?

PAULINE. / Is this back to usury?

EMMA. No, I'll be with you / in a moment.

IAN. Without it being work?

EMMA. Eruv.

PAULINE. What, and if you go too far they cut your hands off?

MARTIN. Eruv?

EMMA. It's called an Eruv. It's a line around a place.

IAN. Just for Jewish people.

EMMA. Which, if you're Orthodox, you can't go beyond if it's the Sabbath. As you well know.

NASIM. Mrs Goodman-Lee.

MARTIN. And Beth Din courts mediate on civil issues. Like the Sharia courts. Things like dowries and divorce.

EMMA. As you well know.

PAULINE. Well, that's all right then.

EMMA. But the point is, if you're asked the question, / do you want...

PAULINE. Dowries and divorce.

EMMA. ...to live in accordance with the values of your faith, or not?

NASIM. Mrs Goodman-Lee.

EMMA. How can you say no? Yes, Nasim, what can I do for you?

PAULINE. So, you're a lesbian Muslim, resident in part of Ponders / End –

NASIM. I am in class with Mr Pritchard.

IAN. Why Ponders End?

EMMA. You *were* in class. How did it go?

MARTIN. Why Ponders End?

NASIM. I have problem with this class.

EMMA. Well, it's entirely voluntary. It has a substantial Bangladeshi population. It's there to help you prep for your exam.

MARTIN. So does Tower Hamlets.

NASIM. Mr Pritchard has streak.

EMMA. What?

PAULINE. All I'm saying is...

NASIM. He has streak on his head.

EMMA. I know, but will he listen to a girl?

MARTIN. In fact, Qur'anic divorce law was extraordinarily liberal for its time.

NASIM. You know my meaning.

PAULINE. I'm sorry?

EMMA. 'Streak' is like 'view' or 'value'.

PAULINE. 'For its time'?

EMMA. Many meanings. It can mean something in your hair.

PAULINE. I'm sorry, 'for its time'?

EMMA. But you can have a funny streak, or a generous streak, which is surely true of Toby Pritchard.

PAULINE. Which is, remind me, what?

NASIM. Or also –

EMMA. Or a vicious streak.

PAULINE. The seventh century?

NASIM. Or another kind of streak.

EMMA. I don't know what you mean.

IAN. And aren't there Jews in Israel…

NASIM. He has a streak.

EMMA. / Yes, we've agreed that.

PAULINE. Yes, I think there are.

NASIM. In two ways.

IAN. / Jewish Orthodox, in Israel…

EMMA. I don't know what you mean.

NASIM. I am so very sorry, please, / but you know what I mean.

EMMA. I'm sorry, but you don't know that.

IAN. You know, who throw stones at buses where the women are not kept in separate places.

NASIM. You know that.

EMMA. It doesn't matter what I know, or don't know. Sorry?

IAN. – who throw stones at buses where the women are not separated.

MARTIN. And attack gay pride.

EMMA. The college has clear guidelines on discrimination.

PAULINE. So you're saying that's all right?

EMMA. We can't discriminate in any way –

IAN. No…

EMMA. – on the grounds of race, religion, gender, ablement or sexuality.

IAN. I'm not saying that's all right…

NASIM. Religion.

EMMA. And that's all we need to say about it.

PAULINE. And you're saying because other people do the same…

MARTIN. No, all that's being said is / that it isn't just –

NASIM. Mrs Goodman-Lee.

EMMA. Yes?

PAULINE. So as long as there's more than one major / world religion –

EMMA. Yes, Nasim?

PAULINE. – which is homophobic –

NASIM. Do you have children?

PAULINE. – then it's fine for the adherents of other major world religions to beat their wives…

EMMA. That's not any of your business.

PAULINE. …:and children, and throw gays off mountains.

NASIM. Then I will pray for you.

EMMA. I'm sorry, what?

NASIM *goes*.

PAULINE. Or put another way, to sum up Emma's argument, there's this Muslim lesbian, trapped in an abusive marriage in East London, but if you can prove that someone somewhere else throws stones at buses then it's fine to leave her there.

EMMA. My argument? Why is it suddenly my argument?

PAULINE. Well, you tell me.

Scene Thirty-Six

ESOL class. TOBY *and* JASMINKA.

JASMINKA. You want I tell my hopes and plans? I come in as au pair in Bromley but the pay is not so fair enough and Mr Henderson does not keep himself to himself. But when I leave this place I borrow maybe bit too much and end up you know how it is. But now I go to English class on Tuesday run by group of ladies who teach me personal empowerment and how to say that I am five foot five inches, 30-C bust, and I not do kissing, Greek or anything without a condom. Also I can make funny talk for cut down time you're in my mouth. And I think now I say all these things, why not I learn bit more good English so I can get British passport and go work with my cousin's friend who runs tourist agency in Prague and sod this for a game of soldiers.

TOBY. Terrific. But maybe... not the condom. Or the mouth. Or in earshot of Nasim.

JASMINKA (*gun gesture to ear*). Uh... 'earshot'?

Scene Thirty-Seven

Home Office. Consultation. All three HISTORIANS *and a* 1ST
CIVIL SERVANT *with a notebook.*

3RD HISTORIAN. Of course, many of our vaunted ancient liberties are actually quite recent gains.

2ND HISTORIAN. Or, put another way, the rights of freeborn
Englishmen are actually rights that other freeborn Englishmen have tried to keep from them for most of history.

3RD HISTORIAN. But nonetheless it is possible to see a progression of what you could describe as British values –
freedom, fairness, decency – which have been fought for,
won and kept across the centuries.

2ND HISTORIAN. So the Swiss aren't fair? The Peruvians
indecent? The South Africans don't value liberty?

3RD HISTORIAN. Along of courses with warm beer, invincible suburbs and old maids peddling off to Evensong.

2ND HISTORIAN. And please, not John Major's fucking old
maids and warm beer.

1ST HISTORIAN. In fact, the old maids were George Orwell.
He wrote the piece in 1940. Perhaps it's worth remembering
what was going on, in the skies above the suburbs, and the
mansions, and the terraced houses, with their front doorsteps
and garden fences and perhaps their glass or two of beer.

2ND HISTORIAN. The truth is, that it's all made up.

3RD HISTORIAN. The truth is, every country is invented.

1ST HISTORIAN. The truth is, if you need to teach it, you
don't know it any more.

1ST CIVIL SERVANT. Well, then. Thanks.

Scene Thirty-Eight

Workplace canteen. CHONG, DEREK, JOSHUA *and* CHLOE.

DEREK. Paris Hilton. Abi Titmuss. Pamela Anderson. And Sharon Stone.

CHONG. I need my book.

JOSHUA. What?

DEREK. You have to guess the question.

JOSHUA. Everybody knows that.

DEREK. Chong don't know that.

CHONG. I am off break now.

CHLOE. Hey. Which of the following British entrants came second – not first, second – in the Eurovision Song Contest?

DEREK. Chlo.

CHLOE. Cliff Richard.

DEREK. Chlo.

CHLOE. Lulu.

DEREK. Fucking hell.

CHLOE. Pearl Carr and Teddy Johnson. Matt Monro. And the winner is…

Suddenly, DEREK *starts singing a football chant, to* The Addams Family *theme.*

DEREK (*sings*). Your sister is your mother
    Your father is your brother
    You all fuck one another
    One happy famil-ee.

To the tune of 'The Red Flag', encouraging JOSHUA *to join in:*

    Up your arse
    Up your arse
    Just stick your blue flag
    Up your arse.

To the tune of 'That's Amore', CHLOE joining in:

> When the ball hits the net
> Who's the scorer I'll bet
> It's Zamora…

To the tune of 'Bread of Heaven'. JOSHUA joins in:

> Does the social, does the social
> Does the social know you're here?
> Does the social know you're here?

CHLOE. Uh… is this a question?

DEREK. Which two of the preceeding chants could not be sung by supporters of Chelsea Football Club?

JOSHUA. Oh, for fuck's sake, Derek…

CHLOE. Yeah, Derek. Koreans probably play table tennis. Give Chong / a break.

CHONG. Well, Zamora is striker for West Ham. And Chelsea flag blue so I don't think somehow Chelsea fan say, 'Stick a blue flag up my arse.'

Pause. JOSHUA, to the tune of 'Ti-yi-yippy-ippy-ay':

JOSHUA. It's all gone quiet over there
It's all gone quiet over there…

DEREK. OK. Which of the following England managers / was not also manager –

During this, JOSHUA picks up CHONG's book.

CHONG. And in two-oh-two world cup, you are knock out in quarter final by Brazil, Michael Owen score in first half but Rivaldo equalise and Ronaldinho score in fifty minute. We lose to Germany in semis one-nil but you're use to that. If citizenship test all on football I am now Duke of Edinburgh.

CHLOE. See, I tell yer, you need to follow the international game…

JOSHUA. I never get the fucking Queen.

DEREK. Yeah, but not / Korea.

JOSHUA. I never get the fucking Queen.

DEREK. I beg your pardon?

JOSHUA. I mean, she's head of government but she don't run the country. And she's head of the Church of England, but she don't wear a funny hat.

CHLOE. Well, actually…

DEREK. She's head of state.

CHLOE. She's what?

DEREK. The head of state's not the head of government. It's like signing laws, and greeting people, and riding round in coaches.

CHLOE. And the Church?

DEREK. I dunno about the fucking Church.

JOSHUA. Three-quarters of the British population believe in God. How many go to church?

CHONG. I'm off break now.

JOSHUA. I know. See you later.

He gives CHONG *his book.* CHONG *goes out.*

DEREK. Later?

JOSHUA. How many go to church?

Scene Thirty-Nine

Child's bedroom. TETYANA *and* MUNA *at the computer.* MUNA *is checking the book for answers.*

TETYANA. Ten per cent? Only ten per cent of people go to church?

MUNA. B. Yes. Saints' days.

TETYANA. So Patrick Day for Irish only and St Andrei for Scottish.

MUNA. Andrew.

TETYANA. But Valentine for everyone. For everyone must love.

MUNA. And Mother's Day.

TETYANA. Because everyone has mother.

MUNA. Yes.

TETYANA. Muna has two mother. Mother and stepmother.

MUNA. Yes.

TETYANA. Next question is hurrah Great British Const/itution.

MUNA. My daddy wants you to be a Muslim.

  Pause.

TETYANA. Yes. Yes, but I don't do that.

MUNA. He says you can dress up in my mummy's clothes.

TETYANA. Too hot, I think. I think I don't do that.

MUNA. Why don't you want to be a Muslim…?

TETYANA. Because I have my own faith, from my mummy. Is called Christian Orthodox. Is hard if you one thing since so many years to change.

MUNA. My daddy says that you can change.

TETYANA. Your daddy want it how it was in Pakistan.

MUNA. I want to change. I don't want to be a Muslim.

  Slight pause.

TETYANA. Muna must not say that…

MUNA. At school they shout at me and say I want to kill people on the buses and my name is Miss Bin Liner.

TETYANA. Muna must not say that…

MUNA. I want to be the toxy thing like you.

  Pause.

TETYANA. Let's do more questions.

MUNA. I want to be the toxy thing.

TETYANA. No, Muna must be Daddy's girl.

MUNA. But I am your girl too.

TETYANA. Yes, you are my girl too.

Slight pause.

Let's do more questions. Yes?

MUNA. OK…

TETYANA. It's fun.

MUNA. OK.

TETYANA. Let's not have boring British Constitution. Ask me something from *Life in UK*.

Scene Forty

Child's bedroom/Home Office. TETYANA, MUNA *and a* MINISTER.

MINISTER. To be honest, the whole thing was very slippery. One lot of media felt you can't be British unless you can list the Plantagenets and recite Gray's 'Elegy'. The other lot was sceptical about the tests in principle.

TETYANA *opens the book and hands it to* MUNA.

TETYANA. Something, anything.

MINISTER. But our real problem was that nobody could agree what British history was. So we decided not to test on history at all.

MUNA (*reading*). 'Check that you understand the key terms and… vocabulary, for this chapter.'

TETYANA. Yo.

Scene Forty-One

Workplace canteen. DEREK *and* CHLOE *watch* JOSHUA *go through the checklist with* CHONG.

JOSHUA. Birth parent.

CHONG. Yes.

JOSHUA. Step-family.

CHONG. Yes.

JOSHUA. Molestation.

CHONG. Think so.

JOSHUA *molests* CHONG.

Yes.

JOSHUA. Gap year.

CHONG. From school to uni.

JOSHUA. Yes. Binge-drinking.

CHONG. Yes…

CHLOE. What's 'binge'?

CHONG. Is very much.

DEREK. All relative.

JOSHUA. Addictive substances.

CHONG. Is heroin cocaine amphetamines.

JOSHUA. And ecstasy and cannabis.

CHLOE. All relative.

JOSHUA. Politics, party politics, fundraising, burglary.

DEREK. Same fucking thing.

JOSHUA. Mugging, racism and terrorism.

CHONG. Mugging?

JOSHUA *mugs* CHONG.

Yes.

Scene Forty-Two

Child's bedroom. MUNA *is testing* TETYANA *from the* Life in the UK *handbook*.

MUNA. In order to marry, each partner must be a years of age.

TETYANA. Eighteen?

MUNA. No, sixteen. 'Living Together.'

TETYANA. Well, this is naughty people.

MUNA. 'These days many couples in the UK live together without getting married.'

TETYANA. Tut-tut. Next?

MUNA. 'Same-sex partnership.' Ships.

TETYANA. I think we leave that. Next?

MUNA. Divorce.

Slight pause.

'In order to divorce... a couple must prove to a court that their marriage has – irre... irre – '

TETYANA. 'Irretrievably broke down.'

MUNA. 'And he or she must prove one of the following:'

TETYANA. Yes, I know this. It is a thing they call adultery or unreasonable behaviour or if they live apart or if one partner has desert.

MUNA. What is desert?

Slight pause.

TETYANA. Sometimes in restaurants it how they say your afters.

MUNA. What is desert?

TETYANA. I say. New subject please.

MUNA. 'Do citizens of EU member states have the right to travel to and work in any EU country if they have a valid passport?'

TETYANA. Maybe we go to splendid British Constitution now.

MUNA. What is desert?

Scene Forty-Three

Workplace canteen. DEREK *and* CHLOE *watch* JOSHUA *going through the book with* CHONG.

JOSHUA. Reasons why you can be dismissed from work.

CHONG. Be late, cannot do job, refuse to join a union.

JOSHUA. No, you can refuse to join a union. Sexual harassment.

CHONG. Rude remarks, things you say to make uncomfortable, touching or sexual demand.

JOSHUA. Dead right.

CHLOE (*to* DEREK). I hope you're noting all this down.

JOSHUA. Now, neighbours. What to do if you have a problem with your neighbour.

DEREK. Like if he molests or mugs you or dumps used needles on your step.

CHONG. If you cannot solve by talking, speak to landlord. Keep full record. If necessary you can take to court and have evicted.

JOSHUA. Yes.

DEREK. Yes.

CHLOE. Welcome to our world.

CHONG. Yes.

Scene Forty-Four

Child's bedroom. MUNA *is testing* TETYANA.

MUNA. More recently, de-volved admin-istrations have been set up.

TETYANA. Yes?

MUNA. In different places.

TETYANA. I think… Ireland and London.

MUNA. Um… yes. Is the British Consti –

TETYANA. – tution.

MUNA. Is it written down in any single document?

TETYANA. Well, I should say so.

MUNA. Hey, good call.

TETYANA. I do so well. My trainer.

MUNA. Who is the head of state of the United Kingdom?

TETYANA. The head of state?

MUNA. Correct.

TETYANA. Prime minister…

MUNA. Yes. That's it.

TETYANA. Or maybe the Archbishop of whatever is the place.

MUNA. Um…

TETYANA. Or maybe it is Queen Elizabeth.

   Pause.

   Give me the book.

MUNA. No.

TETYANA (*grabs at it*). Give me the book.

MUNA. No.

TETYANA. Give me the book or I tell your daddy you don't want to be a Muslim.

MUNA *hands over the book*.

(*Looking at the book*.) 'Queen Elizabeth the Two is the head of state of the United Kingdom'. Oh, she is also 'the monarch or head of state for many countries in the Commonwealth.' What is the Commonwealth, I wonder very much, I don't think. I also wonder very much why Muna lie to Tetyana.

MUNA. I don't lie.

TETYANA (*reads*). 'The British Constitution is not written down in any single document.'

MUNA. You lie to me.

TETYANA. I lie to you?

MUNA. You say this is just a quiz.

Pause. Door slam.

The book says it's a test to be a British citizen.

AZIZ (*offstage*). Tina!

TETYANA. A quiz, a test.

AZIZ (*offstage*). Tina, where are you now?

MUNA. I think if you pass this test you can desert.

TETYANA. That's silly.

AZIZ (*offstage*). Tina!

MUNA. Then tell Daddy what you're doing…

Pause.

AZIZ (*offstage*). Tina, where are you?

TETYANA (*calls*). I'm with Muna! We do homework! Do you want to join us?

Pause.

MUNA. So. This is a test?

TETYANA (*calls*). I'll be down there in few minute!

MUNA. So. This is a test?

TETYANA. Well…

MUNA (*picks up document*). This is the certificate which says my mummy was married to my daddy. Why have you taken this from Daddy's drawer?

TETYANA. OK. This is a test. I take it on computer at a centre. Now we must make two promise.

MUNA. What?

TETYANA. I promise, most sincerely, that whatever happen, Tetyana and Muna stay together. I cross my heart. I swear on *Life in the UK*.

MUNA. And the other promise?

TETYANA. This is Muna's promise. That she help me so I pass this test.

Pause.

MUNA *picks up the book. Opens it, flips through it, as if idly. Eventually:*

MUNA. Who appoints the members of the House of Lords?

TETYANA. The people!

MUNA. No, they are appointed by the Queen on the advice of the prime minister.

TETYANA. But I thought UK is… Hey-ho.

Scene Forty-Five

Documentary. Citizenship blog.

'VERY WORRIED'. Hi, I just found in the last week that from 2nd April 2007 you need to pass the citizenship test to get Indefinite Leave to Remain in the UK. My husband arrived on a marriage visa. Every time he looks at the Life in the UK book he breaks out in a sweat, feels dizzy, and feels like throwing up.

Scene Forty-Six

Home Office. Documentary: Life in the UK. *Two* CIVIL SER-VANTS, *with the* 1ST *and* 2ND EDITIONS *of* Life in the UK.

1ST CIVIL SERVANT. We did revise the book, after consulta-tions. It was felt to be too complicated.

2ND CIVIL SERVANT. A little inaccessible.

1ST EDITION. 'The English like to think that theirs is the mother of parliaments.'

2ND EDITION. 'The English Parliament was not unique.'

2ND CIVIL SERVANT. And we did feel we needed to respond to changes in the political atmosphere.

1ST EDITION. 'The police are there to be helpful.'

2ND EDITION. 'All good citizens are expected to help the police.'

1ST CIVIL SERVANT. Overall, the aim of the revisions was to give more emphasis to national belonging.

2ND CIVIL SERVANT. Hence the bit we put in about Red Nose Day.

Scene Forty-Seven

ESOL class. EMMA, HALIMA, BABA, RANJIT, DRAGOSLAV *and* NASIM.

EMMA. So, would anybody like to tell us why they came to Britain?

Slight pause.

If 'why' is the question, what word do we expect in the answer?

BABA. / Because.

DRAGOSLAV. Because.

Enter SAMIR.

EMMA. Exactly… Maybe, Nasim?

SAMIR. So sorry.

NASIM. Why and how I came to Britain?

SAMIR. I have meeting.

EMMA. Had. Yes.

NASIM. I came because you want my father to work here.

EMMA. 'You', meaning?

NASIM. Britain, the UK. I come by British Airways.

Pause.

EMMA. Right. Anybody else?

Pause.

SAMIR. I come here from Iran.

EMMA. Terrific. Halima, ask Samir why and how he came to Britain from Iran.

HALIMA. Uh…

EMMA. Start by asking why he left.

HALIMA. Why are you leave Iran?

EMMA. 'Why did you leave?' Did. Past word.

SAMIR. I am very interesting to come to England.

EMMA. Interest*ed*, but was there a reason why you left Iran? 'I left Iran, because…'

SAMIR. I left Iran because they make me soldiers. They must maybe make me soldier.

EMMA. So you left because they wanted you to go into the army. Halima. Ask Samir how he travelled.

HALIMA. How you travel?

EMMA. How *did* you travel?

SAMIR. I pay money and I go with truck.

EMMA. In a truck. And what countries did you / go through?

SAMIR. No. No.

Gestures, low.

EMMA. I don't…

SAMIR. Not in truck. With wheel.

EMMA. You mean, underneath. With the spare wheel.

SAMIR. Spare wheel.

EMMA. And this is… all the way to England.

SAMIR. No.

EMMA. So…

SAMIR. In Lebanon we stop by men they want more money.

EMMA. And what happens?

SAMIR. I no more money.

EMMA. Yes?

SAMIR mimes hitting.

SAMIR. So I hit.

EMMA. You hit someone…

SAMIR. No, I hit.

He mimes hitting himself.

EMMA. Someone hits you.

He stops.

That is, 'I am hit.' It's the passive. It is done to you. But it's a yesterday word.

SAMIR. Yesterday?

EMMA (*thumb*). Before.

BABA. Was hit.

EMMA. Yes. I *was* hit. Where? Somewhere else. Why 'was'? Because it is not happening now. Now you are learning English for Speakers of Other Languages, at a college here in London.

RANJIT. Britain. The UK.

EMMA (*hands out cards*). Indeed. So what makes Britain British? Cards with pictures.

(*To* NASIM.) I'm so very sorry. Of typical things that they say that British people do. Do?

SOME. Action.

EMMA. Action. Eating potatoes out of newspapers. Standing politely in long lines. Visiting big cold wet places in the summer.

Handing a card past NASIM.

Pouring intoxicating liquors down our throats. And I'd like you to get in pairs and discuss what these actions are and if you think that British people really indulge in these bizarre behaviours.

General bafflement.

Bizarre. Weird. Crazy.

NASIM *holds up the card she's been given.*

NASIM. What is this card?

EMMA. Well, it appears to be a meal. I would say – it's an English breakfast.

NASIM. Yes.

EMMA. How can this be problematical?

NASIM. What is this thing?

EMMA. I believe it is a picture of a sausage.

NASIM. Sausage pig.

EMMA. Not necessarily.

NASIM. And this?

EMMA. Is a slice of bacon. Now, is this a problem?

NASIM. Pig is unclean.

EMMA. Not to British people. That's why we're / discussing –

NASIM. You ask me discuss this go against religion.

Slight pause.

EMMA. Then have another card.

NASIM. But you say we discuss all these cards.

Slight pause.

EMMA. Yes.

NASIM (*re:* HALIMA). We must not discuss this.

EMMA. Then it is fine if you go outside while we discuss the cards.

NASIM. What d'you say?

EMMA. I am saying, if you don't want to discuss the cards, then you can leave the room.

NASIM. It is *haram* to discuss unclean.

Puts down the card and waits.

You know *haram*?

EMMA. Of course.

NASIM. It means…

EMMA. Forbidden.

NASIM *goes and stands by the door.*

NASIM (*Arabic*). *Ma fina nebhath bi halmawdoa.* [So it is not possible to discuss it.]

Pause.

EMMA. Nasim, you know we have a rule in / college...

NASIM (*Arabic*). *Mamnoa aleina annabhath bi heik mawdoa ya ja maa!* [We are not allowed to discuss it!]

HALIMA *stands and joins* NASIM. SAMIR *doesn't move*.

Clear rule at college, on religious discrimination, here in London Britain the UK.

NASIM *and* HALIMA *go out.* EMMA *picks up the abandoned cards.*

EMMA. The government did a list of British things. Stonehenge. *Punch and Judy.* Cups of tea. A sculpture called *The Angel of the North.*

SAMIR. *Punch and Judy?*

EMMA. Puppets. Dolls. Man and woman.

Fighting gesture.

DRAGOSLAV. Fighting.

EMMA. Yes. And there was a prime minister, called John Major.

RANJIT. Like Winston Churchill?

EMMA. Only in that respect. And he said Britain was cricket, warm beer, I think he said 'invincible suburbs'.

The fighting mime and a defiant stance.

BABA. No surrender.

EMMA. No surrender. And old women bicycling to church. To their religion. People thought it was all pretty out-of-date.

Slight pause.

Because of course it should have been fruity little Cabernets and mountain-biking to invincible three-bedroom cottages in Umbria.

Slight pause.

DRAGOSLAV. Emma. You are homesick.

EMMA. Yes.

Slight pause.

Forgive me please. As we all know, British people read the *Sun* and eat sausages and stand in queues and play the game.

Scene Forty-Eight

Home Office. The MINISTER *and the two* CIVIL SERVANTS.

1ST CIVIL SERVANT. And of course, we studied what they did abroad.

MINISTER. I went to Canada.

1ST CIVIL SERVANT. The first big section of *A Look at Canada* is about taking care of the environment.

2ND CIVIL SERVANT. The good Canadian separates his trash.

MINISTER. The key thing about the ceremony there is that it's in an informal setting. You know, with a cup of tea.

1ST CIVIL SERVANT. While in the German state of Hessen they proposed asking would-be immigrants how they'd respond if someone said the Holocaust was a folk tale. Or what they'd think if their son said he was homosexual. Oh, and to identify the central motif of a famous landscape painting of a Baltic island.

MINISTER. Hence being referred to as…

2ND CIVIL SERVANT. The Muslim test.

1ST CIVIL SERVANT. While if you want to be Dutch, then you have to watch a DVD of two men walking hand in hand and a topless woman walk out of the sea.

2ND CIVIL SERVANT. We knew the press would ring up people at the Home Office and ask them questions from the test they couldn't answer.

MINISTER. So we decided the new citizen should understand the institutions he or she would need to navigate in Britain.

1ST CIVIL SERVANT. In other words…

MINISTER. We wanted the information to be useful.

2ND CIVIL SERVANT. In essence, I suppose, we came to the conclusion that the most important element of Britishness is the need and capacity to find a dentist.

Pause. The MINISTER *goes out.*

1ST CIVIL SERVANT. Six hundred and fifty-five, all told. We do think, as the cost of naturalisation, that is quite horrendous.

2ND CIVIL SERVANT. But we are huge fans of the ceremony.

Scene Forty-Nine

Documentary. Citizenship blog.

'SALIM SHARIF'. I can understand everyone's point of view. However, if some one wants to become Japanese or Chinese citizen (for example) or even want to become the citizen of your own country where you are originally from, wouldn't you normally expect that applicant to know the language, system, culture and laws before he/she becomes the citizens?

Scene Fifty

Child's bedroom. TETYANA *slumped over computer.* MUNA *has come in.*

MUNA. Tetyana. What's the matter?

  TETYANA *shakes her head.*

  What's the matter?

TETYANA. Terrible.

MUNA. What's terrible?

TETYANA. Test place is next door to Madjit's.

MUNA. Madjit?

TETYANA. Madjit is Daddy big supplier…

MUNA. So?

TETYANA. So I can walk in there?

MUNA *smiles and goes out.*

Muna! You make me promise now!

Scene Fifty-One

Documentary. Citizenship blog.

'STEPHEN'. I'm fed up with people complaining about this test. I'm British, I've paid Tax all my life, i deserve to live here. Further more, what does it matter that some British people can't pass the test! We don't have to! We were born here!

Scene Fifty-Two

Dinner party.

EMMA. So you're saying, being Muslim is incompatible with being 'British'?

MARTIN (*to* IAN). Emma teaches many Muslims.

PAULINE. I'm saying that if you wear foreign clothes and speak / a foreign language –

EMMA. 'Foreign clothes'?

PAULINE. – and live in ghettoes –

MARTIN (*to* IAN). They bring gulab / jamun and halva –

EMMA. 'Ghettoes'?

MARTIN. – and evince great bafflement about her status and opinions.

PAULINE. Who was it said, we're 'sleepwalking into segregation'?

EMMA. Oh, and British people don't like keeping themselves to themselves?

PAULINE. All I'm saying is…

MARTIN. Now she teaches citizenship. An almost perfect way to destroy two thousand years of British culture, history and tradition.

PAULINE. Well, precisely.

EMMA. Martin…

IAN. Strictly speaking, British history / doesn't –

EMMA (*to* IAN). I teach English with twenty hours of citizenship content.

MARTIN. Emma doesn't want to gatekeep for the goverment.

IAN. In fact, Britain as a state / is only –

EMMA. At least it means they don't all have to sit a jolly quiz on a computer about public holidays and the powers of local government and who's head of the Church of England. Ian?

PAULINE. They shouldn't know who's head of the Church of England?

EMMA. Ian, you were saying.

IAN. In fact, it isn't who you think it is.

PAULINE. Or when Christmas is? Or if you have to send your kids to school? Or who picks up the rubbish? I mean, how easy do you want to make it?

EMMA. Or perhaps: what is the minimum wage and how far are you prepared to work below it? Name three crustaceans which you'll risk your life for off the coast of Lancashire?

Oh, and list the services you're prepared to perform on behalf of Albanian sex-traffickers in order to retrieve your passport?

Pause.

Sorry, I…

MARTIN. Emma.

EMMA. Sorry. Ian, you were saying.

IAN. All I was saying was, that when you say 'British culture', what you actually mean…

Pause.

But I guess that's what you'd expect me to say.

PAULINE. You know that 'Finland' is a Swedish word? The Finns call Finland 'Suomi'.

MARTIN. Emma. Do you have a problem with your class?

Scene Fifty-Three

Dinner party. Soliloquy: IAN.

IAN 2. So what am I describing? A country that is joined up to another country and constantly referred to by its name. Having been invaded by that other country and incorporated into it 'for its own sake'. Whose ancient and venerable traditions were invented by that other country, banned, and then expropriated by its royal family. Oh, and which is sitting on a sea of oil. From which the other country generously agrees to rescue it. As it has done so often elsewhere in the world.

He turns to the others.

But I guess that's what you'd expect me to say.

Scene Fifty-Four

ESOL class. EMMA *and* TOBY. *During their conversation, the class assembles:* DRAGOSLAV, RANJIT, NASIM, BABA *and* ELIMA. HALIMA *is absent.*

TOBY. Today, Halima is unwell. But Jasminka has returned from – holiday. She has brought baklava. And we are debating… human rights?

EMMA. We are debating human rights. Shabina Begum – a schoolgirl – was allowed by her school to wear the shalwar kameez, but she wanted to wear the full-length jilbab instead. Let's check out our initial opinions. Hands up those who think she had the right to wear exactly what she wanted.

NASIM *and* BABA *put up their hands.*

And who thinks the school was right to say she had to wear the uniform?

DRAGOSLAV, RANJIT *and* JASMINKA *vote.*

(*Handing out playing cards.*) Aha. Now I would like us to discuss this question. If you get a red card, you argue the side you agree with. If you get a black card, you argue the side you don't agree with. Does everybody understand? Now, we start with the high numbers. Any tens? Nines?

RANJIT *puts his hand up.*

Ah, Ranjit. Should the school have the right to stop the girl wearing the full-length gown?

RANJIT. Um…

EMMA. You can even stand up, if you like.

RANJIT *stands.*

RANJIT. People of London.

EMMA. Marvellous.

RANJIT. If you ask me my opinion, I say, we can all say what you want, we wear also what we want. And religious right are most important for diversity and equal opportunity. No difference for race or class or creed. So the school must allow all girls to wear religious clothing. This is how it is here in UK. This is I must say not my own opinion.

EMMA. I would not have known.

She leads the applause.

Now, any eights?

JASMINKA. I have too nine.

EMMA. Ah, Jasminka. So, what's your view?

JASMINKA. I...

TOBY *goes and looks at her card and whispers to her.*

EMMA. You understand?

JASMINKA. I am OK with this.

EMMA. That's wonderful.

JASMINKA *stands.*

JASMINKA. This is my opinion, fellow people.

EMMA. Yo.

JASMINKA. I say the school it is correct in this thing. If not, you are Muslim, your friends say you must say this or that, or maybe wear this or that, and if not they say you are bad Muslim.

Slight pause.

Friends and you family and father too I think. I know such case. And that is my opinion.

EMMA. Brilliant.

Applause.

Any more nines? Or eights? Or sevens?

NASIM *hand up.*

Ah, Nasim. Please. The floor is yours.

NASIM. Well, in my view this is very typical, Mrs Goodman-Lee.

EMMA. Don't tell me, tell the group.

NASIM. If you wear miniskirt, this is OK and brilliant. Free of speech. If you wear low-cut top, this quite terrific.

RANJIT. This is not the same, I think.

EMMA. Shh, shh.

NASIM. You wear immodest clothe this will be all free choice and human rights. You wear religious clothe and this is oh your father and brother beat you. Why you say this?

EMMA. I don't say this.

NASIM. Why you say this?

EMMA. Tell the class.

NASIM. Why is it – very big thing –

EMMA. Such a big thing.

NASIM. – so a very big thing…

TOBY. So important.

NASIM. Why it is so important. That she cannot wear jilbab because she wants to wear jilbab.

Pause.

RANJIT. She has black card. She speaks the wrong way.

EMMA. Yes, I know.

NASIM. Why do you know?

EMMA. I gave you the black card deliberately.

NASIM. Why?

EMMA. To see if you could argue the opposing point of view.

NASIM. To see if I play up the game.

EMMA. To see if you can see the other side. Some people say that's what being British is about.

NASIM. Oh yes?

EMMA. Seeing the other person's point of view.

NASIM. I think to give black card is discrimination. I will make complaint about you, Mrs Goodman-Lee.

EMMA. Against me. Yes, I know.

Pause. NASIM *goes out.*

Jasminka has brought everyone baklava.

EMMA *follows* NASIM *out.*

Scene Fifty-Five

ESOL class. EMMA *and* NASIM.

EMMA. You realise you have no hope of succeeding.

NASIM. You do not like to hear this.

EMMA. You have no legitimate complaint about the class today.

NASIM. You try to make me attack my religion.

EMMA. I do nothing of the kind.

NASIM. You say I must take pictures home.

EMMA. No, I did / not.

NASIM. You make me learn by perverted person.

EMMA. You cannot say / that.

NASIM. For my religion that is great abomination.

EMMA. Under the guidelines of the college you are not allowed to / say that.

NASIM. So free of thinking.

EMMA. You can think it but you cannot say it.

NASIM. You must not say what you think.

EMMA. Not in the college.

NASIM. But OK you tell me say what I don't think.

EMMA. I'm sorry, we shouldn't have this / conversation.

NASIM. Mrs Goodman-Lee, I think you will not defend the thing you love because you do not love it very much.

EMMA. I'm sorry, I don't see it that way.

NASIM. Mrs Goodman-Lee. What if I say I want to kill all Christian people?

EMMA. You cannot say that in the college.

NASIM. You don't say 'this terrible attack on my religion'?

EMMA. I may not be a Christian.

NASIM. Are you a Christian?

EMMA. No I am not a Christian.

NASIM. What is your name till marry?

EMMA. I'm not sure that's any of your / business.

NASIM. Why is your name two pieces?

EMMA. Double-barrelled. I don't see that's anything / to do with –

NASIM. What if I say it might be good to kill Jews with car bombs? What if I say the 7/7 people are Fab Four? Is that not your business?

Pause.

EMMA. I don't… think you think that.

NASIM. Although I must not speak, you know what I think.

EMMA. I don't think that you have to kill yourself or anybody else to prove what you believe in.

NASIM. I march against Denmark cartoons in London. I say, 'Death to the insulter of the prophet.'

EMMA. Did you?

NASIM. I am nine in Egypt when the fatwa against Salman
    Rushdie. I wish of anything I had been adult then in England
    the UK.

EMMA. Really?

NASIM. Although I understand for you it look so different.

EMMA. Yes.

Scene Fifty-Six

Dinner party.

PAULINE. All I'm asking is, what you felt like, on the greatest
    demonstration in the history of time, what you felt marching
    ten abreast through central London, demanding that two dem-
    ocratic countries shouldn't overthrow a criminal dictator,
    shoulder to shoulder with people who'd come from Birm-
    ingham on women-only buses? Who disguise themselves as
    pillar boxes on the grounds that this is the only way to fend
    off uncontrollable male sexual desire? Whose religion justi-
    fies the killing of apostates? Who believe in burning books
    and hanging if not beheading people? And that there's a
    secret worldwide Jewish conspiracy? How you felt – you feel
    – about being on the same side as these people?

Scene Fifty-Seven

ESOL. Soliloquy: NASIM.

NASIM 2. I was nine when the fatwa against Salman Rushdie
    happened. I was carried to the Midan al-Tahrir in Cairo on
    my father's back. He said we were protesting for our
    brothers and our sisters in a place very far away called
    England. Where our people are attacked with petrol and
    called 'Pakis', and our Prophet, peace be upon Him, most
    cruelly abused. We protest to say to our people, there in
    England: you are no longer underground. You are not

alone but part of worldwide family. To show how many of us there are.

Pause.

And d'you know what my father said to me? If you ever doubt your faith, if you're ever lured by materialism and impurity, if you're ever tempted to give up the fight for justice, brotherhood and the sacred land, then remember how we felt that day.

NASIM *turns to* EMMA.

Although I understand for you it look so different.

Scene Fifty-Eight

Dinner party.

PAULINE. Just because the other side was your country and America?

EMMA. So we shouldn't agree with Muslims on Iraq?

PAULINE. Well, on balance, I am marginally hostile to the creation of Islamic states through acts of terror.

IAN. Well, of course, you could say, the invasion / did in fact –

MARTIN. And what you call 'terrorism' might look different if you see yourself as occupied by / a foreign –

PAULINE. Ah, yes. Israel. Tell me, when you tell your students, your numerous and halva-bearing Muslim students, that you haven't got a child, do you mention your divorce?

EMMA. It's not any of their business. What has that to do with Israel?

MARTIN. In fact, Muslim divorce law / is –

PAULINE. Its connection with the other thing that you might mention.

Pause.

IAN. I think I've kinda lost what's going / on here –

EMMA. We're half-Jewish.

IAN. Yes, I know.

PAULINE. So, is that the half you tend to mention?

Pause.

IAN. Look, maybe…

MARTIN. In fact, the college guidelines / state –

EMMA. In fact, if you ask them why they want to live here –

PAULINE. Yes, what – what happens if you ask them why they want to live here?

Pause.

EMMA. I'm sure to you it's all baloney.

Scene Fifty-Nine

Dinner party. Soliloquy: EMMA.

EMMA 2. Live and let live. Takes all sorts. Fair play. You don't have to carry papers. You aren't under constant security surveillance. You don't have to tell people who you are or where you live. The police can't stop and search you without reason, or lock you up unless they charge you. You can say just what you want to say, however offensive or outrageous. Teachers don't report on your opinions to the government, and policemen aren't allowed to shoot you in the street.

Slight pause.

That's what they come for. The very things our government is trying to take away from us because they're here.

EMMA *turns to* PAULINE.

I'm sure to you it's all / baloney.

PAULINE. You know the difference between us? You think it, and I say it.

Scene Sixty

Top-floor room. JAMAL *has been testing* MAHMOOD.

JAMAL. So this is what you want? You want like you belong to a country where the most important moral principle is that drunken slags shouldn't use unlicensed minicabs?

MAHMOOD. I said, it's for / me dad.

JAMAL. And half the kids think Mount Everest's in Europe. And the other half can't read.

MAHMOOD. Ay, well…

JAMAL. And three-quarters say as they believe in God. But only one in ten does owt about it.

Pause.

Where are the values? Where is the submission to a higher purpose? Where are the great stories of its past achievements? Where are its tales of valour and of sacrifice?

MAHMOOD. They're in the first bit of the book. Like, they don't test you on that bit.

JAMAL. Nar. They test you on how to get a driving licence. And addictive substances. Oh, and 'same-sex partnerships'.

He tosses the book down and makes to go.

MAHMOOD. So you can't be a Muslim if you're gay?

JAMAL. I have a meeting now.

MAHMOOD. Or you can't be a Muslim if you don't say it's a sin?

JAMAL. Chicken, tomato or asparagus?

MAHMOOD. I'll have a pizza.

JAMAL. Pizza?

MAHMOOD. Ay.

JAMAL. You want pizza?

MAHMOOD. Ay.

Slight pause.

In fact, you've no need for a separate licence, s'long as you share the same address. 'Less you rent a room at that address.

Slight pause.

I can have asparagus. Like, as a topping. If you like.

Scene Sixty-One

Child's bedroom. TETYANA *stands, ready to go out.* MUNA *stands opposite, holding a pile of black cloth.*

TETYANA. You must go to school.

MUNA. It's half term.

TETYANA. Till you're sixteen. But prescriptions free for sixty years and over.

Pause.

If Daddy asks, where am I?

MUNA. Lidl on the Alcester Road.

TETYANA. You get it?

MUNA. Here.

TETYANA *goes and takes the black cloth, which is the chador and niqab, a full-length black gown with scarf and veil.*

TETYANA. People not elected to half of democratic parliament so why? – Beats me. You cannot be sack for being homosexual but you can for sexual harrassing. You must never climb into unlicensed taxi. R-eighteen means very filthy film. Your mummy wear this thing?…

MUNA. Yes.

TETYANA. She die.

MUNA. My daddy say.

TETYANA. Say what?

MUNA. She must wear it.

TETYANA. Why?

Pause.

Why?

MUNA *mimes hitting herself.*

He hit her?

MUNA *shakes her head.*

She hit herself?

MUNA *shakes her head.*

She cut herself?

MUNA *nods.* TETYANA *attaches the veil.*

Nobody know. Wish me good luck.

Scene Sixty-Two

ESOL class. MARTIN *and* EMMA.

MARTIN. So, have you read it?

EMMA. No, I haven't.

MARTIN. You'll obviously have to read it.

EMMA. Yes.

MARTIN. You do know the procedure?

EMMA. Sort of. I've not been up / against –

MARTIN. Technically, she's made a complaint to your team
leader, whose response was not to her satisfaction, and to the
head of school ditto, and so I'm obliged to mount a formal
hearing. At which she has a friend, and you can have the union.

EMMA. What does it say?

MARTIN. I imagine the 'friend' has had a hand...

EMMA. What does it say?

MARTIN. An incident about some pictures you required her to take into her house.

EMMA. I didn't 'require' her to do anything.

MARTIN. She tried to speak to you about a voluntary teacher, / who apparently –

EMMA. About Toby Pritchard. She complained about his hair.

MARTIN. I'm sorry?

EMMA. He'd streaked his hair.

MARTIN. And...

EMMA. Guess.

MARTIN. It says here that he insisted on interrogating her about her beliefs in a / tutorial...

EMMA. Is Toby summoned to the show trial?

MARTIN. No, the complaints are against you. And it's not a show trial.

EMMA. Oh, of course not. I've got the UCU...

MARTIN. And there's excluding her from class.

EMMA. Excluding her from class?

MARTIN. She says you told her to leave class.

EMMA. She was refusing to participate.

MARTIN. Yuh, you were discussing pubs and bacon.

EMMA. We were discussing aspects of the British character. To which she had / objections.

MARTIN. And you told her to leave the room.

EMMA. I told her she could leave the room. While we / discussed –

MARTIN. She says you said, 'You can leave the room.' She says 'can' is sometimes a 'maybe word'? But the way you said it sounded more like an injunctive. What she calls 'a bossy word'.

EMMA. What I call 'a bossy word'.

MARTIN. Of course, the issue is fundamentally / religious…

EMMA. The issue is that Nasim didn't want / to participate –

MARTIN. It says here, she didn't want to advocate a view she didn't hold.

EMMA. Martin, I handed out some playing cards. As I've done a hundred times.

MARTIN. Yuh. Playing cards.

Slight pause.

She calls it bullying.

EMMA. Bullying?

MARTIN. She or the friend have obviously read the / guidelines.

EMMA. So have I.

MARTIN. I think the argument… is that it all adds up. The pictures then the bacon then the playing cards.

EMMA. You know I'm thinking I might jack this in.

MARTIN. Emma.

EMMA. Move to Cambridge.

MARTIN. Emma.

EMMA. Apparently they get a lovely class of English Language student in the / Fens –

MARTIN. You don't have to do that.

EMMA. I don't have to do anything.

MARTIN. You so don't have to do that.

EMMA. Yes, when did that happen?

MARTIN. When did what…

EMMA. Putting the word 'so' in funny places in the sentence.

MARTIN. I suppose it's an emphatic. So much, implied. When I was a revolting student, everything was 'too much'. As, of course, much of it was.

EMMA. Even the wonders of ninety-sixty-fucking/-eight –

MARTIN. Yes, that's the point.

EMMA. You're saying it's the same?

MARTIN. I'm saying that students have always protested against the curriculum.

EMMA. Yes, but about what isn't in it, not / what is –

MARTIN. Schoolkids always object to what they're made to wear.

EMMA. So the jilbab's the equivalent of jeans?

MARTIN. We used to moan about how conservative the students had become…

EMMA. But, Martin, that's the point. They *are* conservative. You think they're peace and love.

MARTIN. I don't think we were peace and love.

EMMA. They're fire and brimstone.

MARTIN. Well, 'burn, baby, burn'.

EMMA. But of course we back the underdog. Whatever they believe, / and whoever they support.

MARTIN. I'm saying, we can't be Victorian philanthropists. Choosing between the deserving / and the undeserving poor.

EMMA. Martin, this isn't somebody who fails to tug their forelock with sufficient vigour. This is somebody who asks me…

Pause.

MARTIN. What are you saying?

EMMA. It doesn't matter.

MARTIN. What are you saying?

EMMA. It doesn't matter.

MARTIN. Tell me what you mean.

EMMA. Something she said.

MARTIN. What did she say?

Pause.

Did she threaten you?

EMMA. Not me.

MARTIN. What did she say?

Pause.

EMMA. I signed a letter to the *THES*, protesting about teachers being asked to spy on students.

MARTIN. But, Emma…

EMMA. It was just a provocation. Tit for tat.

Pause.

MARTIN. Look, Emma. You will win this.

EMMA. Are you supposed to / say that?

MARTIN. At the very worst…

Slight pause.

EMMA. What? What, 'at the very worst'?

Slight pause.

A reprimand? A warning?

MARTIN. As I say.

EMMA. When she was nine, she wanted to burn books.

MARTIN. We wanted to burn everything.

Scene Sixty-Three

Soliloquy: MARTIN.

MARTIN 2. What am I describing? An oppressive and aggres-
sive state, whose agencies are not subject to the rule of law.
Persecution of ethnic and religious groups. Capital punishment, liberally applied. Hostility to free speech, pluralism of
opinion. A belligerent and rapacious foreign policy.

So why did I and the best part of two million others march
through London to protest against its overthrow?

Now, what am I describing? A state which doesn't yet exist,
whose principles include all the above, plus rampant homo-
phobia, the subservience of women, pursuing global domina-
tion by campaigns of foreign conquest by a mighty leader
subject only to the will of God.

So why did I march side by side with people who want to
bring such a state about?

The answer comes: because although we hate these things
with every fibre of our being, the thing we hate even just a
little bit more is America.

But of course this isn't true. In fact, like anybody of my gen-
eration, I love America. The movies. Jazz. San Francisco.
Greenwich Village. For Christ's sake: Bob Dylan and Frank
Zappa are American.

In fact, the only bit I don't like is the middle.

The bit that hates gays and burns books and loves the death
penalty. Believes that women should be subject to their hus-
bands. And that it should conquer foreign countries, and be
led by men who think they do God's will.

Scene Sixty-Four

ESOL class/Child's bedroom.

EMMA. The first thing to say. To those of you who are taking your ESOL test. I shall miss you. But I hope… Although I hope you pass, I shall miss you.

TETYANA. It is not so far away.

MUNA. King's Cross.

TETYANA. It is to Euston ninety minutes on the train. And then five-minute walk away.

EMMA. The second thing. For those of you who go on learning English. Ing, ing, ing.

MUNA. You will come back?

EMMA. I have sad news…

TETYANA. Sure, I….

EMMA. Aaah.

MUNA. You will come back?

EMMA. However, you will be in the capable and equally remunerated hands of Mr Chlebowski.

  TETYANA *does a practice curtsey.*

TETYANA. Muna so wonderful my trainer.

  She kisses MUNA *and goes out.*

EMMA. Because…

  HALIMA *and* SAMIR *come in to* EMMA.

  Because…

SAMIR. Mrs Goodman-Lee. So sorry?

EMMA. No. No, I was…

HALIMA. You prepare.

EMMA. Yes, I prepare.

HALIMA. Like actor theatre.

EMMA. Yes.

Enter NASIM.

SAMIR. Mrs Goodman-Lee. I take ESOL test.

EMMA. You will take. Yes. I am supremely confident.

HALIMA. We pass, we go to council place near King's Cross for ceremony.

EMMA. I know that too. However, I do have to tell / you –

SAMIR. We can take some person. Hold the camera.

EMMA. Hm?

HALIMA. We liking you to come with us.

EMMA. Uh… why?

SAMIR. Because by you I see my nieces and my nephew and my brother.

EMMA. Uh… why?

SAMIR. For although I view so much important being British citizen, for me however it is so I fly to United Arab Emirates and I meet my family who quick cross the straits of Hormuz from Iran.

Pause.

EMMA. So you… so that's why you need a British passport.

SAMIR. A little bit bizarre. To learn 'ing' words and 'although however' and *The Angel of the North*. And English breakfast.

EMMA. All to see your niece and nephew in Dubai.

Scene Sixty-Five

Workplace canteen/Child's bedroom. JOSHUA, DEREK *and* CHLOE *singing to the tune of 'The Conga'.* MUNA *is still in her room.*

CANTEEN GROUP (*sings*). Chong's only fucking done it
    Chong's only fucking done it
    La-la-la-la. La-la-la-la.

MUNA (*calls*). What do I say? If Daddy asks me where you are? Do I tell him you're in King's Cross? What do I say?

Scene Sixty-Six

West Yorkshire. MAHMOOD *has found* JAMAL.

JAMAL. Mahmood.

MAHMOOD. Jamal.

JAMAL. I thought you was / in London.

MAHMOOD. I came up. 9.30 from / King's Cross.

JAMAL. King's Cross. Look, I'm / a bit –

MAHMOOD. You ever come to London?

JAMAL. Sometimes.

MAHMOOD. Gets me certificate on Tuesday. I can take a guest.

    Pause.

JAMAL. Uh, I…

MAHMOOD. You saved me from myself.

    MAHMOOD *looks at his watch.*

    (*Arabic.*) *Hel tarab an tosaly maee?* [Do you want to pray with me?]

JAMAL. What you say?

MAHMOOD. Do you want to pray with me?

After a moment, JAMAL *kneels.* MAHMOOD *has a notebook.*

Which of these statements is correct? (A) 'There is no compulsion in religion.' (B) 'Whoever changes his religion shall be executed.'

JAMAL. Eh?

MAHMOOD. Remember. I were studying.

(*Reads.*) 'Who fights in the way of Allah, be he slain or be he victorious, on him we shall bestow a vast reward.' Or 'Whoever kills an innocent, it is as though he has killed humanity entire.'

JAMAL. I've no time for this right now.

MAHMOOD (*finding a passage in a marked page of the Qur'an*). 'Prophet, make war on the unbelievers and the hypocrites. Hell shall be their home.'

(*Another marked passage.*) 'God has promised the men and women who believe in Him gardens watered by running streams, in which they shall abide for ever.'

JAMAL. Look…

MAHMOOD. Sounds like some high.

JAMAL. Look…

MAHMOOD (*holds out the open page of the Qur'an, marked with a Post-it note*). Guess that's why you've marked it up.

Pause.

So you gets me clean. And some other lads. And you goes to college and you stops the discos and you have 'em close the place for Friday prayers. Or maybe you dress up smart and cool and you campaign for the creation of a caliphate throughout the Muslim lands. Or p'raps you download clips of people sawing people's heads off. Or maybe you go off to Pakistan and join 'the real fighters'.

Slight pause.

I know as it were Bernie.

JAMAL. What were?

MAHMOOD. Bernie, as tells my auntie to tell you as I needs saving from myself.

JAMAL. Bernie?

MAHMOOD. She can't even read. But she were right about me needing saving. As you said, if I carried on that way, I'd die.

Pause.

So tell us. When they've done the video? What happens if they change their mind?

Scene Sixty-Seven

Citizenship ceremony.

ASSISTANT. I swear by Almighty God that, on becoming a British citizen, I will be faithful and bear true allegiance to Her Majesty Queen Elizabeth the Second –

RESPONSE. Her Majesty Queen Elizabeth the Second –

ASSISTANT. – Her Heirs and Successors according to law.

RESPONSE. – Her Heirs and Successors according to law.

ASSISTANT. I will give my loyalty –

The door crashes open. A middle-aged Pakistani man, AZIZ, bursts into the room.

AZIZ. Stop this.

MAYOR. Uh, what?

AZIZ. I know what's happening.

ASSISTANT. Please, what –

People running. Babies screaming.

MAYOR. You can't –

AZIZ. Where are you?

ASSISTANT. What do you want?

He tears off FATIMA*'s veil.*

MAYOR. No, you can't –

AZIZ. I know what you are doing here.

MAHMOOD. Hey, pal –

AZIZ. I know what you are doing now. Where are you?

AZIZ *sees* TETYANA.

Tina!

TETYANA. Aziz.

AZIZ *turns and rushes at* TETYANA. JAMAL *brings him to the ground.*

JAMAL (*Arabic*). *Tawaqafa. Eh daá.* [Stop it. Keep calm.]

AZIZ. Keep off me.

JAMAL (*Arabic*). *Escot la tataharak.* [Keep quiet. Don't move.]

AZIZ. What you saying?

JAMAL. What's up, man? What's going off?

AZIZ. This is my wife. She does this so she can desert me.

JAMAL *looks up at* TETYANA, *who shrugs.*

ASSISTANT. Look…

MAHMOOD. Have you done? Like, is she a citizen?

ASSISTANT. No, not until…

MAHMOOD. Then finish it.

AZIZ. But, Tina…

ASSISTANT. I will give my loyalty to the United Kingdom –

AZIZ. But, Tina…

TETYANA. I will give my loyalty to the United Kingdom –

AZIZ. Tina, I lie to / you.

ASSISTANT. And respect its rights and freedoms.

TETYANA. And respect its rights and freedoms.

AZIZ. I cannot say we are / sham marriage.

ASSISTANT. I will uphold its democratic values.

TETYANA. I will uphold its democratic values.

AZIZ. I say we are sham marriage I go to / prison for deception.

ASSISTANT. I will observe its laws faithfully –

TETYANA. I will observe its laws faithfully –

AZIZ. Tina, you do not need / to do this.

ASSISTANT. And fulfill my duties and obligations as a British citizen.

TETYANA. And fulfill my duties and obligations as a British citizen. What you say?

ASSISTANT. That's it.

AZIZ. I say I lie to you.

MAHMOOD. The certificate?

TETYANA. You lie to me?

AZIZ. They cannot send you back.

ASSISTANT. Name?

TETYANA. Tetyana Ismael. What?

AZIZ. If you desert they cannot send you back.

TETYANA. So why you lie to me?

The ASSISTANT REGISTRAR *goes to the box.*

AZIZ. I lie because I need you. Muna need you.

MAHMOOD. The certificate.

AZIZ. Tina, I need it how it was.

The ASSISTANT REGISTRAR *finds the certificate.*

TETYANA. What, how it was in Pakistan?

AZIZ. No. Here.

The MAYOR *moves in front of the flag and the Queen's portrait.*

MAHMOOD. Do you have a camera?

Everybody has a camera. The ASSISTANT REGISTRAR *hands the* MAYOR *the certificate. The* MAYOR *presents the certificate to* TETYANA.

MAYOR. Many congratulations.

TETYANA (*curtseying*). Thank you...

Flashes from the camera. JAMAL *lets* AZIZ *stand.*

AZIZ. Tina, I need you. Muna need you. If you leave, we die.

Pause. TETYANA *looks at* AZIZ.

TETYANA. You stay home. You help with Muna homework. You tell everyone in Newcastle and Oldham who I am. I can leave at any time. It can't be how it was. I do no self harm. I am now British citizen.

Pause.

AZIZ (*to everyone*). If she leave, we die.

MAYOR (*prompt, whispers, gesturing at the others*). 'I will give my loyalty...'

ASSISTANT. Yes.

MAHMOOD. Nobody's going to die. Nobody's going to harm themselves. To save one person is to save humanity entire.

ASSISTANT. I will give my loyalty to the United Kingdom –

Scene Sixty-Eight

Testing the echo.

IAN. 'So there is, as I have argued, a golden thread that runs through British history... of the individual standing firm against tyranny.'

FARZANA. A then-future Prime Minister, January 2006.

SYRUS. 'Our tolerance is part of what makes Britain, Britain. So conform to it; or don't come here.'

FARZANA. A then-current Prime Minister, December 2006.

SUSHIL. In British theatres, it is considered rude to be on time.

ROBERT/SIRINE. 'Surely, after all, our system should recognise – and penalise – behaviour that clearly shows disregard for the values that help us all live together.'

FARZANA. Two Ministers, June 2007.

IAN. On first entering the Tube, it is customary to shake hands with every passenger.

ROBERT. 'Everyone should sit down once a year and think how lucky they are to be British.'

FARZANA. One of those Ministers, June 2007.

KIRSTY. In Scotland, men's lavatories are identified by a picture of a kilted man.

ROBERT. During your visit, you should not fail to try out the famous echo in the Reading Room of the British Library.

TERESA. So, what am I describing?

ROBERT. Tradition, rolling back through centuries.

IAN. A military ethos.

SYRUS. God's law, at the very heart of civic life.

IAN. The idea that certain actions are required of the good citizen.

FARZANA. Charity.

KIRSTY. Clean living.

SIRINE. Modesty.

FARZANA. The garden fence, the front doorstep.

SUSHIL. Minding your own business…

FARZANA. Keeping yourself to yourself.

SIRINE. The notion, nonetheless, of a sacred land of brotherhood and justice, somewhere in the future.

JAMAL. 'Till we have built Jerusalem…'

KIRSTY. For now though: Duty.

ROBERT. Obligation.

SYRUS. Sacrifice.

TERESA. Which of these statements is correct?

MEN. That's how we are.

WOMEN. That's how they ought to be.

HALF. That's how they are.

OTHER HALF. That's how we were.

EMMA. Although –

The End.

Other Titles in this Series

Stella Feehily
DUCK
O GO MY MAN

Debbie Tucker Green
BORN BAD
DIRTY BUTTERFLY
RANDOM
STONING MARY
TRADE & GENERATIONS

Ayub Khan-Din
EAST IS EAST
LAST DANCE AT DUM DUM
NOTES ON FALLING LEAVES
RAFTA, RAFTA...

Tony Kushner
ANGELS IN AMERICA – PARTS ONE & TWO
CAROLINE, OR CHANGE
HOMEBODY/KABUL

Stephen Jeffreys
THE CLINK
A GOING CONCERN
I JUST STOPPED BY TO SEE THE MAN
THE LIBERTINE

Conor McPherson
DUBLIN CAROL
McPHERSON: FOUR PLAYS
McPHERSON PLAYS: TWO
PORT AUTHORITY
THE SEAFARER
SHINING CITY
THE WEIR

Bruce Norris
THE PAIN AND THE ITCH

Steve Thompson
WHIPPING IT UP

Steve Waters
FAST LABOUR
THE UNTHINKABLE
WORLD MUSIC

Nicholas Wright
CRESSIDA
HIS DARK MATERIALS *after* Pullman
MRS KLEIN
THE REPORTER
THERESE RAQUIN *after* Zola
VINCENT IN BRIXTON
WRIGHT: FIVE PLAYS

A Nick Hern Book

Testing the Echo first published in Great Britain in 2008 as a paperback original by Nick Hern Books Limited, 14 Larden Road, London W3 7ST, in association with Out of Joint

Testing the Echo copyright © 2008 David Edgar

David Edgar has asserted his moral right to be identified as the author of this work

Cover portraits by Graham Michael
Cover design by Ned Hoste, 2H

Typeset by Nick Hern Books, London
Printed in the UK by CPI Bookmarque, Croydon CR0 4TD

A CIP catalogue record for this book is available from the British Library
ISBN 978 1 85459 553 9